True Tales
of
Raging Waters

Henry Billings

Melissa Stone Billings

STECK-VAUGHN
ELEMENTARY · SECONDARY · ADULT · LIBRARY

A Harcourt Company

www.steck-vaughn.com

Acknowledgments

Editorial Director: Stephanie Muller
Senior Editor: Kristy Schulz
Associate Director of Design: Cynthia Ellis
Design Manager: Alexandra Corona
Production Coordinator: Rebecca Gonzales
Media Researcher: Claudette Landry
Page Production Artist: Dina Bahan
Cover Production Artist: Alan Klemp

Cartography: Pp. 4–5, 7, 15, 23, 31, 39, 47, 55, 63, 71, 79, 87, 95, MapQuest.com, Inc.
Illustration Credits: Pp. 13, 21, 29, 37, 45, 53, 61, 69, 77, 85, 93, 101, Eulala Conner
Photo Credits: Cover (background) ©Richard T. Nowitz/CORBIS; front cover (inset) ©Galen Rowell/CORBIS; back cover (spot) ©PhotoDisc; p.1 ©Richard T. Nowitz/CORBIS; pp.3, 6 ©PhotoDisc; p.8 ©Robert Holmes/CORBIS; pp.9, 10 ©CORBIS; p.14 ©Michael S. Yamashita/CORBIS; p.16 ©Bettmann/CORBIS; p.17 ©Paul Almasy/CORBIS; p.18 ©Bettmann/CORBIS; p.22 ©Superstock; p.24 Courtesy Bates College; pp.25, 26 Courtesy Dan Stockwell; p.30 ©T. Orban/SYGMA; p.32 ©Anthony Suau/Liaison Agency, Inc.; p.33 ©T. Orban/SYGMA; p.34 ©Anthony Suau/Liaison Agency, Inc.; p.38 ©Ken Krakow/Liaison Agency, Inc.; p.40 ©C. Weiner/Liaison Agency, Inc.; p.41 ©Ken Krakow/Liaison Agency, Inc.; p.42 ©C. Weiner/Liaison Agency, Inc.; p.46 ©Anne Nosten/Liaison Agency, Inc.; p.48 ©P. Robert/SYGMA; p.49 Corbis; p.50 ©P. Robert/SYGMA; p.54 ©CORBIS; pp.56, 57 ©PhotoDisc; p.58 AP/Wide World Photos; p.62 ©Paliani Mohahn/Sipa Press; p.64 Corbis; p.65 ©Sydney Herald/Sipa Press; p.66 AP/Wide World Photos; p.70 ©CORBIS; p.72 Reuters/Stringer/Archive Photos; pp.73, 74 ©AFP/CORBIS; p.78 ©Noel Quidu/Liaison Agency, Inc.; p.80 AP/Wide World Photos; pp.81, 82 ©S. Wood/Royal Navy/Sipa Press; p.86 © Nick Rains; Cordaiy Photo Library Ltd./CORBIS; p.88 Reuters/David Gray/Archive Photos; p.89 ©Newspix; p.90 ©SYGMA; p.94, 96 AP/Wide World Photos; p.97 ©Pascal Fayolle/Sipa Press; p.98 AP/Wide World Photos; p.108 ©PhotoDisc; p.108 ©Corbis; p.108 ©Michael Andrews/Earth Scenes; p.109 ©Breck P. Kent/Earth Scenes; p.109 ©Johnny Johnson/Animals Animals; p.109 ©PhotoDisc.

ISBN 0-7398-2391-4

3 4 5 6 7 8 9 10 DBH 04 03 02

Contents

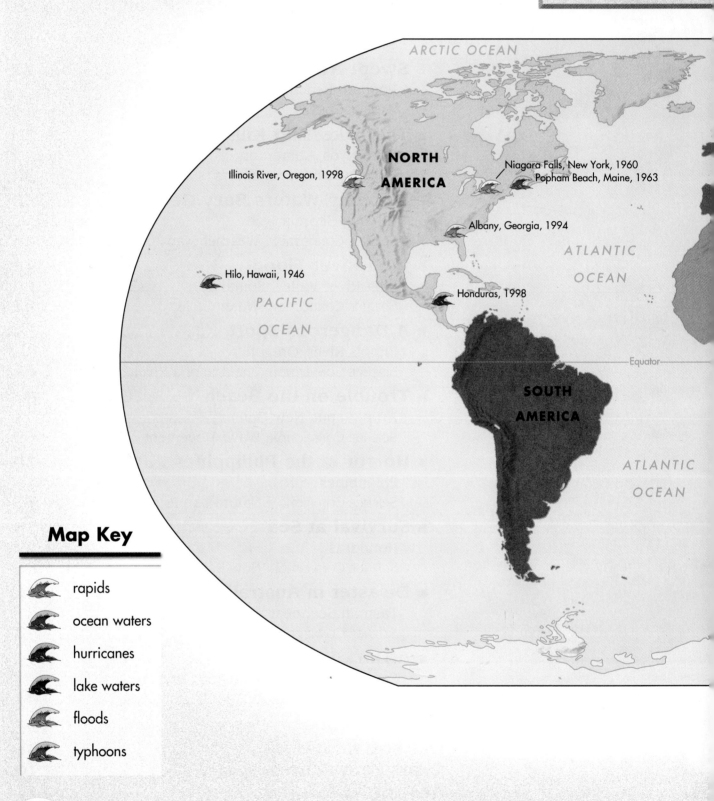

ARCTIC OCEAN

NORTH AMERICA

Illinois River, Oregon, 1998

Niagara Falls, New York, 1960
Popham Beach, Maine, 1963

Albany, Georgia, 1994

ATLANTIC OCEAN

Hilo, Hawaii, 1946

PACIFIC OCEAN

Honduras, 1998

Equator

SOUTH AMERICA

ATLANTIC OCEAN

Map Key

- rapids
- ocean waters
- hurricanes
- lake waters
- floods
- typhoons

of
Waters

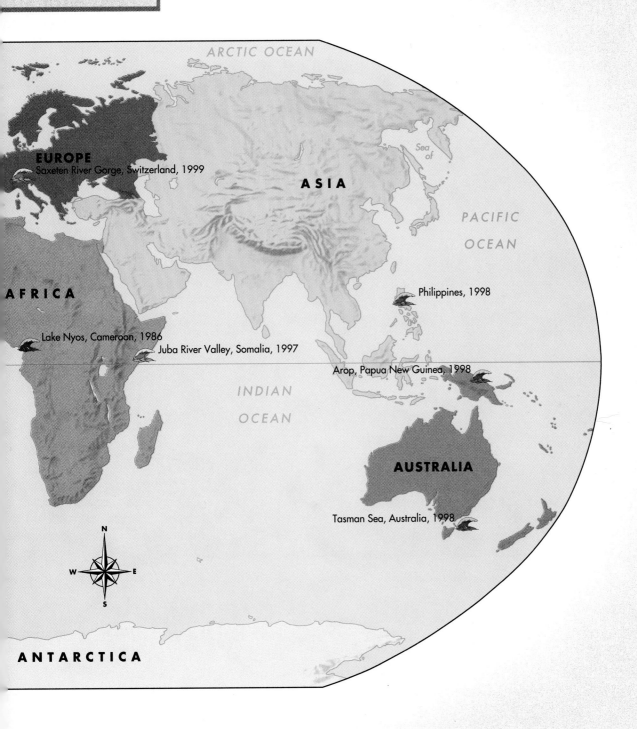

ARCTIC OCEAN

ASIA

Sea of

EUROPE
Saxeten River Gorge, Switzerland, 1999

PACIFIC

OCEAN

AFRICA

Philippines, 1998

Lake Nyos, Cameroon, 1986

Juba River Valley, Somalia, 1997

Arop, Papua New Guinea, 1998

INDIAN

OCEAN

AUSTRALIA

Tasman Sea, Australia, 1998

ANTARCTICA

Big Waves Hit Hawaii

What an odd sight it was. All along the shore, the sea was suddenly **disappearing**. People in Hilo, a city on the island of Hawaii, had no idea what was going on. But when they looked out across the north shore on April 1, 1946, they were shocked. Land that had always been underwater was now in the sun. Fish were lying everywhere, flopping around on the wet sand. The ocean looked like a bathtub after someone had just pulled the plug.

The Rising Sea

Tuck Wah Lee was working near the shore at the time. He heard someone yelling. Lee went outside to see what was happening. He saw the water in the **bay** draining away. Other people who were working near the bay began rushing down onto the beach. They wanted to gather the fish that were lying there. Lee didn't join them. He decided to get a better look at the bay. So he climbed a nearby tower.

That move probably saved Lee's life. As he reached the top of the tower, he looked out at the bay again. "I saw a brown wall of water coming in," he later said. "The wall got higher and higher. The whistling sound that came with it got louder and louder."

The wall of water was a giant wave. Within seconds, Lee saw it sweep away everything below him. It washed away the buildings where Lee worked. It washed away the people on the beach. It almost swept away Lee himself. The water came within two feet of him.

People in Hilo did not know that a giant wave was headed their way.

Meanwhile, 20 miles away, a high school girl named Leonie Poy was getting ready for school. She saw all her school friends running down along the shore. Poy and her brother, Will, hurried to join them. When they got to the beach, they saw that there was no water.

Poy had a strange feeling that something was very wrong. She and her brother raced back to their home. Their father agreed that trouble was coming. He rushed them into the car. Then he quickly drove for higher ground.

As Leonie Poy looked out the back window of the car, she saw the sea suddenly rise. A huge wave crashed over the trees and homes along the shore. The wave swept up many of her friends. They never had a chance. Twenty of Poy's friends drowned in the huge wave.

Speed and Power

The wave that Lee and Poy saw really began far out to sea. It started up near Alaska. That was 2,500 miles north of Hawaii. There, deep under the Pacific Ocean, an **earthquake** took place. The land at the bottom of the sea shifted down sharply. Water rushed into the new opening caused by the shifting ground. That made the **surface** of the ocean rise and fall creating waves.

The power of the moving water moved south. As it traveled, it gained speed. The deeper the water, the stronger and faster the rise and fall became. By the time the moving water reached Hawaii, it was traveling about 400 miles per hour.

Moving water this powerful is often called **tidal waves**. But that is wrong. Waves have nothing to do with **tides**. Tides are a normal part of ocean life. They happen every day. The right word to use is **tsunami**. This word comes from Japan. It means "**harbor** wave." The Japanese chose this word because the waves usually hit hard along harbors and shores. The tsunami that headed toward Hawaii was huge.

A tsunami is no trouble as long as it stays out at sea. Someone on a ship might not even feel a tsunami passing by. The trouble starts when a tsunami comes close to land. There the water is not very deep. So the front of the wave starts to slow

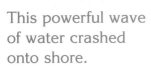

This powerful wave of water crashed onto shore.

down. But the back is still moving fast. Water near the back spills on top of water at the front. The power of the water makes the tsunami grow higher and higher. The huge wave that Lee and Poy saw was as high as 55 feet. That made it taller than a four-story building.

A tsunami is usually one big wave. But sometimes it can be followed by five or six other giant waves. As each wave nears the shore, it pulls in the **surrounding** water. That's why Lee and Poy saw the water near the shore disappearing.

Life and Death

Lee and Poy both lived through the tsunami. But 159 people were killed. Almost everyone caught by the wave died. Luckily, that is not likely to happen again. **Scientists** have found a way to tell when an earthquake might cause a tsunami. They can warn people ahead of time. In 1946 it took the tsunami four hours to reach Hawaii. If people had been given a warning, they would have had time to run away.

People looked at their ruined city after the tsunami was over.

Read and Remember — Finish the Sentence

Circle the best ending for each sentence.

1. Tuck Wah Lee saw the water near the shore _____.
turn black   disappear   fill with stones

2. The giant waves began near _____.
Mexico   the South Pole   Alaska

3. Tuck Wah Lee climbed a _____.
tree   tower   wall

4. Leonie Poy's father drove _____.
toward the beach   to higher ground   to a ship

5. Poy and Lee both _____.
drowned   lived   got lost

Think About It — Find the Main Ideas

Underline the two most important ideas from the story.

1. Leonie Poy's brother was named Will.

2. In 1946 an earthquake caused a tsunami to hit Hawaii.

3. Someone on a ship might not feel a tsunami pass by.

4. More than 150 people were killed by the giant tsunami that hit Hilo, Hawaii.

5. People saw fish flopping on the wet sand.

Focus on Vocabulary — Match Up

Match each word with its meaning. Darken the circle beside the correct answer.

1. harbor
   ○ place for ships   ○ strong wind   ○ kind of boat

2. surface
   ○ top layer   ○ hard swim   ○ a man's face

3. tsunami
   ○ Japanese ship   ○ island in Hawaii   ○ giant waves

4. earthquake
   ○ shaking of the ground   ○ special day   ○ loud noise

5. tides
   ○ long sticks   ○ rocks   ○ daily movement of sea

6. surrounding
   ○ shaking   ○ all around   ○ very cold

7. bay
   ○ city   ○ seawater with land partly around it   ○ river

8. disappearing
   ○ getting big   ○ going out of sight   ○ becoming angry

9. scientists
   ○ students   ○ people who study science   ○ workers

10. tidal waves
    ○ fresh water   ○ high waves near shore   ○ beaches

Giant Waves

Earthquakes can occur under the ocean. This makes the **surface** of the ocean rise and fall, creating waves. When the waves get near the shore, they slow down and can become a giant **tsunami**. They actually pull water away from the shore. The diagram below shows a tsunami. Write the answer to each question.

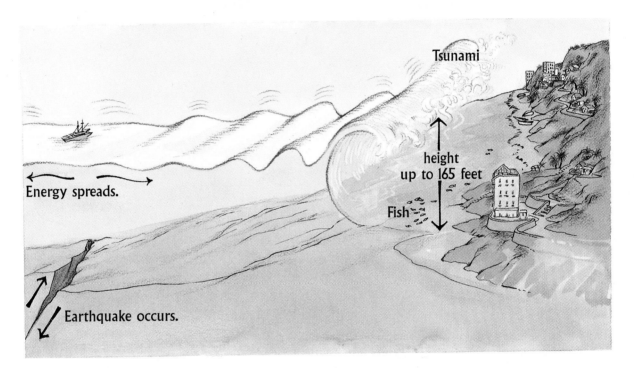

Tsunami

height up to 165 feet

Fish

Energy spreads.

Earthquake occurs.

1. What can happen to fish when a tsunami pulls water away from the shore? _____

2. What happens to the waves when they near the shore? _____

3. What is a giant wave caused by an earthquake? _____

4. How high can tsunamis become? _____

5. Is a tsunami's height highest at sea or near shore? _____

Life and Death at Niagara Falls

It was a hot Saturday afternoon in the town of Niagara Falls, New York. Like everyone else, seven-year-old Roger Woodward had trouble staying cool. So he was happy when Jim Honeycutt showed up. Honeycutt was a family friend. He owned a small fishing boat. On this day, July 9, 1960, Honeycutt offered to take Roger for a boat ride. Roger's seventeen-year-old sister, Deanne, was also invited. Both wanted very much to go. They knew a boat ride would cool them off. They had no idea that it would also put them in great danger.

Heading Toward the Falls

Mr. and Mrs. Woodward agreed to let Roger and Deanne go. But Roger didn't know how to swim. So they made him put on a **life jacket**. Deanne was a good swimmer, so they didn't think she needed one. Still, Jim Honeycutt said there was a second life jacket in the boat just in case.

When they got out on the water, Roger and Deanne had a great time. The wind blew through their hair. **Mist** from the river sprayed their faces. They didn't know where Honeycutt was taking them and they didn't care. "Deanne and I had no idea we were on the upper Niagara River," Roger said.

Jim Honeycutt didn't seem to know that, either. He pointed the boat **downstream**. That meant it was headed right toward the **waterfalls**. These falls are very famous. People come from all over the world to see them. But the falls are also deadly. The water drops 165 feet through the air before reaching the bottom. More than a million gallons of water flow

over the waterfalls every second. This makes the power of the water very strong.

It's not just the falls themselves that are deadly. There are also dangerous **rapids** right before the falls. There the water moves very fast. It crashes over sharp rocks at about 50 miles an hour.

No one knows why Jim Honeycutt headed his boat toward the falls. "Maybe he was just trying to give us a **thrill**," Roger said years later. "Or maybe he just didn't know where he was."

In any case, the boat soon got caught in the strong **current** leading to the falls. Once that happened, they were in real trouble. There was no way that Honeycutt could turn the boat around.

Trying to Stay Alive

As they moved into the rapids, the boat hit a rock. "The boat started moving faster, and Jim couldn't control it," Roger said. Honeycutt yelled to Deanne to put on the extra life jacket. Just as she did so, the boat tipped over. All three people went into the water. Honeycutt was lost in the rapids. His body was later found at the bottom of the falls.

Roger and Deanne tried hard to keep their heads above water. They hit rock after rock as they were swept along. Nearing the falls, Roger lost all hope. "I knew I was going to die," he said.

But luckily he didn't. The water carried him over the falls. But because he was wearing a life jacket, he stayed near the surface of the water. At the bottom of the falls, people pulled him safely to shore. He was the first person ever to go over Niagara Falls and live without being in a special **container**.

A Hero in the Crowd

Deanne Woodward never went over the falls. A man named John Hayes pulled her out just in time. Like hundreds of others, Hayes had been enjoying the view from the **riverbank**. But when he saw Honeycutt's empty boat tumble over the falls, he knew something was wrong. Then he spotted

The fast-moving water carried Roger Woodward over the falls.

Deanne. She was swimming as hard as she could toward shore. But she was less than 100 feet from the falls.

Quickly, Hayes leaped over the railing near the falls. He ran down to the water's edge. Leaning way out over the water, he saw Deanne passing by. "I'll never forget that girl's face as she went by screaming for help and reaching out," Hayes said. He stretched his hand out toward her as far as he could. "Girl!" he yelled. "Come to me!"

By this time, Deanne was just 20 feet from the falls. She made one last **desperate** move to save herself. Somehow she grabbed Hayes's hand. "I only got the first two fingers and thumb," Hayes said. "But she wasn't about to let go." A second man came out of the crowd and helped pull her to safety.

Everyone felt terrible about the death of Jim Honeycutt. But they cheered John Hayes as a hero. They also cheered Deanne and Roger Woodward. As Roger said years later, "The greatest gift is that my sister and I are both still alive."

Roger Woodward was lucky to be alive.

Read and Remember — Choose the Answer

Draw a circle around the correct answer.

1. Who took Roger and Deanne Woodward for a boat ride?

Mr. Woodward   Jim Honeycutt   John Hayes

2. Why did the Woodwards make Roger wear a life jacket?

He couldn't swim.   He was scared.   He was sick.

3. What happened to the boat as it neared the falls?

It ran out of gas.   It tipped over.   It began to leak.

4. What did Deanne grab to save herself?

a tire   a tree branch   John Hayes's hand

5. What happened to Roger after he went over the falls?

He drowned.   He was pulled to safety.   He swam.

Write About It

Do you think people should be allowed to take boats out on the upper Niagara River near the huge waterfalls? Write a paragraph explaining your answer.

_____

_____

_____

_____

_____

_____

Focus on Vocabulary — Find the Meaning

Read each sentence. Circle the best meaning for the word in dark print.

1. Roger Woodward wore a **life jacket**.
   jacket that floats   heavy coat   jacket with snaps

2. Their faces were covered with **mist**.
   dirt from the river   fine drops of water   cuts

3. Jim Honeycutt pointed the boat **downstream**.
   to land   into the flowing water   into the wind

4. The **waterfalls** are very famous.
   rivers   old boats   places where water drops

5. The **rapids** were dangerous.
   animals living in water   steps   fast-moving water

6. At first, the ride was a **thrill**.
   cold feeling   feeling of excitement   tired feeling

7. The boat got caught in the **current**.
   gate   moving water   strong wind

8. Roger Woodward was not in a special **container**.
   box   suit   class

9. John Hayes was on the **riverbank**.
   land at a river's edge   kind of boat   fence

10. Deanne Woodward made one last **desperate** move.
    underwater   nearly hopeless   lonely

Parts of a River

A river is water that flows into another body of water. The place where the river starts is called the **source**. The **mouth** is the place where the river enters the other body of water. Some rivers have **rapids** and **waterfalls**. Study the diagram. Circle the answer to each question.

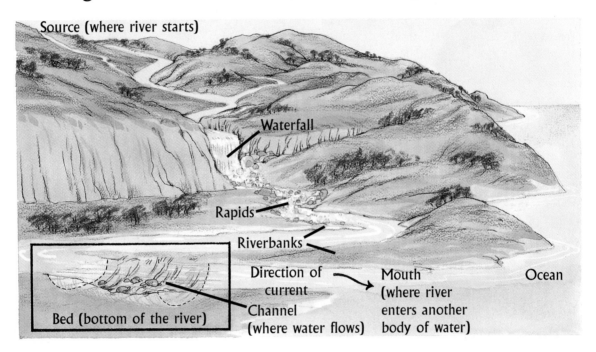

Source (where river starts)

Waterfall

Rapids

Riverbanks

Direction of current

Mouth (where river enters another body of water)

Ocean

Bed (bottom of the river)

Channel (where water flows)

1. Which is the place where a river starts?
   mouth   channel   source

2. What is the bottom of a river called?
   bed   current   rapids

3. What does a river enter at its mouth?
   a mountain   a waterfall   another body of water

4. What part of the river is the riverbank?
   its side   its end   its amount of water

5. Where on the river does water drop down suddenly?
   current   channel   waterfall

Swept Away

Every spring the students at Bates College went to Popham Beach, Maine. There they had a picnic to enjoy the end of school. They played volleyball. They sat in the sun and looked out at the Atlantic Ocean. On May 13, 1963, Stephen Quattropani was one of these students. The day started off well for Quattropani. But before it was over, one of his classmates would be dead. Quattropani himself would almost die.

A Big Wave

During the picnic, Quattropani and some others decided to go to Fox Island. It was next to Popham Beach. When the tide was low, people could walk right out to it. So that's what Quattropani did. A bunch of other students went with him. Among them were Dale Hatch and Dan Stockwell.

On Fox Island, the students climbed a twenty-foot **cliff**. From there they looked out at the roaring ocean. Wave after wave crashed against the rocks below. It was a thrilling sight.

Quattropani wanted a closer look. So he made his way to the bottom of the cliff. Then he climbed a fifteen-foot rock at the water's edge. Quattropani thought he would be safe there. But a big wave washed over the rock. It knocked him off his feet. Then it swept him out into the cold Atlantic Ocean.

Quattropani tried to keep his head above the water. He tried to swim back to land but he couldn't. The pull of the water away from the shore was too

strong. This pull, called an **undertow**, meant that Quattropani could soon be carried far out to sea. He either could die from the cold **temperature** of the water or he could drown.

Trying to Help

Back up on the cliff, Dale Hatch and several other students saw what had happened. They knew they had to act fast to save Quattropani's life. So they grabbed all the clothes they could find. They picked up sweaters and sweatshirts. They tied these together to form a rope. They hoped to throw the rope out to Quattropani and pull him to shore.

The clothes rope wasn't long enough to reach Quattropani from the top of the cliff. So Dale Hatch climbed down toward the water. When he got to a **ledge** near the bottom, he stopped. Then he threw one end of the rope out into the water.

As he did so, another wave came rolling in. It knocked Hatch off the ledge and into the water. Hatch was not a good swimmer. Also, he was dressed in leather boots and heavy clothes. So right away he had trouble keeping his head above water. Now there were two students in danger. It looked like both of them would be dead within minutes.

Saving a Classmate

Dan Stockwell had no idea that something terrible was happening. He was sitting in a quiet spot with his girlfriend. Then someone came running over to him, screaming. Looking out at the water, Stockwell saw Hatch and Quattropani. By then, both men were tiring. They were both being swept away by the dangerous undertow.

Stockwell did not **hesitate**. He was a trained **lifeguard**. He thought he might be able to help. So he rushed down to the water's edge. He took off all his clothes except for his bathing suit. Other students found a volleyball net and cut it up to make a long rope. Stockwell tied one end of the rope around his waist. He gave the other end to friends to hold. Then he dove into the cold water.

Dan Stockwell and his girlfriend on Fox Island

"When I saw Dan get out of his clothes, I started screaming," his girlfriend remembered. "The waves were so high that in the water you couldn't see over the **crest**.... The undertow sucked everything out like a **vacuum**."

Stockwell swam as fast as he could through the rough water. Hatch and Quattropani were in deep water about 35 feet from shore. They were ten feet away from each other. As Stockwell neared them, Hatch disappeared under a wave. Sadly, he did not come back up. His body was found hours later.

Stockwell reached out for Quattropani, who was floating face down. By then Quattropani was **unconscious**. Stockwell held him tight while the students on shore pulled on the rope. As Stockwell and Quattropani were dragged in, Stockwell felt his legs hitting against sharp rocks. It hurt terribly. But he never let go of his classmate.

Once at shore, Quattropani was rushed to the hospital. He had almost died in the water. But happily, he **survived**. He owed his life to Dan Stockwell and the other students who had helped save him from the deadly undertow.

Read and Remember — Check the Events

Place a check in front of the three sentences that tell what happened in the story.

_____ **1.** Stephen Quattropani was washed into the sea near Fox Island.

_____ **2.** The students at Bates College refused to go to Fox Island.

_____ **3.** Dan Stockwell jumped into the water and saved Quattropani.

_____ **4.** Dale Hatch drowned trying to save Quattropani.

_____ **5.** A terrible storm caused the death of a Bates College student.

Think About It — Cause and Effect

A **cause** is something that makes something else happen. What happens is called the **effect**. Match each cause with an effect. Write the letter on the correct blank. The first one is done for you.

Cause	Effect
1. The tide was low, so __**b**__	**a.** he had trouble keeping his head above water.
2. Stephen Quattropani wanted a closer look at the ocean, so _____	**b.** students could walk out to Fox Island.
3. Dale Hatch wanted to save Quattropani, so _____	**c.** he climbed onto a rock at the water's edge.
4. Dan Stockwell needed a rope, so _____	**d.** he climbed down a cliff and threw a rope into the water.
5. Dale Hatch was not a good swimmer, so _____	**e.** students made one out of a volleyball net.

Focus on Vocabulary — Make a Word

Choose a word in dark print to complete each sentence. Write the letters of the word on the blanks. When you are finished, the letters in the circles will tell who was at Fox Island on May 13, 1963.

hesitate	unconscious	vacuum	ledge	cliff
survived	temperature	undertow	lifeguard	crest

1. The students climbed a twenty-foot _____.

   ◯ _ _ _ _

2. Dale Hatch was swept off a _____ near the water's edge.

   ◯ _ _ _ _

3. Dan Stockwell was a trained _____.

   _ _ _ _ ◯ _ _ _

4. Quattropani could not swim because he was _____.

   _ _ _ _ _ ◯ _ _ _ _ _

5. It was hard to see over the _____ of the waves.

   _ _ ◯ _ _

6. The undertow sucked water out like a _____.

   _ _ _ ◯ _ _

7. The _____ of the water was very cold.

   _ _ _ _ _ _ ◯ _ _ _ _

8. The _____ was very strong and dangerous.

   _ _ _ _ _ ◯ _ _

9. Quattropani was lucky he _____.

   _ _ _ _ ◯ _ _ _

10. Stockwell did not _____ to help.

    ◯ _ _ _ _ _ _ _

Ocean Currents

Water that flows in an ocean moves in **currents**. One kind of current flows close to shore. It moves sand from the beach out to the water. Sometimes it builds a **sandbar**. Another kind of current is called a **rip current**, or **undertow**. It returns the water to the ocean. Study the diagram of currents. Write the answer to each question.

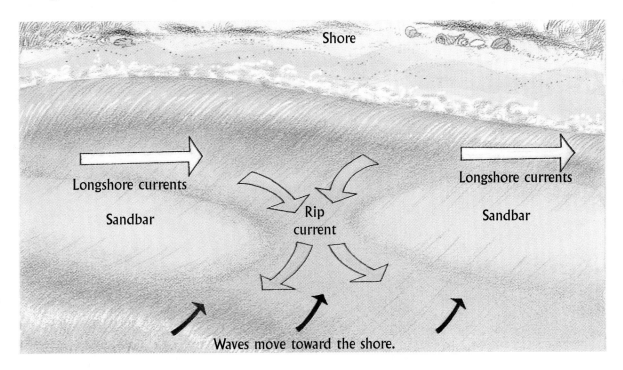

1. Can a current flow near shore? _____

2. What kind of current returns water to deeper parts of the ocean?

   _____

3. What is another word for *rip current*? _____

4. How are sandbars built up? _____

   _____

5. Why do you think a rip current can be dangerous for swimmers?

   _____

The Lake That Kills

In 1999 Gambo Djibril dreamed of going back to live by the lake. He and his family had been in a **refugee** camp for 13 years. Before living in the camp, they had lived near Lake Nyos in the African country of Cameroon. Then in 1986 they had to leave along with 3,500 other people who lived near the lake.

Life in the refugee camp was hard. But at least Djibril and his family were safe. Back at Lake Nyos, no one was safe. The lake looked peaceful. But it still held a deadly secret.

The Lake Explodes

At 9,876 feet, Lake Nyos sits high among some old **volcanoes**. The lake itself is in one of the **craters**. Before 1986, the lake was beautiful. The water was clear blue and very deep. But there was trouble at the bottom of the lake.

Over many years, a deadly gas was building up. This gas is **carbon dioxide**. It usually does no harm to people. In fact, a small amount of it is put in soft drinks to make them bubble. But in very large amounts, carbon dioxide will kill. That's because it is heavier than **oxygen**. So it can push oxygen away. If enough carbon dioxide is in the air, it can push away all the oxygen. Then there isn't any oxygen left for people to breathe.

There was a lot of carbon dioxide on the bottom of Lake Nyos. But no one knew about it. So people saw no danger in settling near the lake. Families like the Djibrils built homes near the water. They grew **crops** and raised cows there.

Then, on August 21, 1986, something **disturbed** the lake. No one knows for sure what happened. There may have been an earthquake under the lake. In any case, the ground under the water shifted. That stirred up the lake. Suddenly, carbon dioxide started to bubble up toward the surface.

At first the gas moved slowly. Then it gained speed and power. At last, it reached the surface. A huge blast of gas and water roared up out of the lake. It was like shaking up a can of soda and suddenly popping it open. Water spilled out of the lake in a great wave. It knocked down all the trees and plants along the shore.

Deadly Gas

But the water wasn't the real problem. The killer was the carbon dioxide. As the gas bubbled out of the lake, it formed a huge cloud. This deadly cloud was 150 feet high. Because the gas was so heavy, it flowed down into the valley like a river. It pushed away all the oxygen.

The people in the village of Lower Nyos did not know that the carbon dioxide was coming. They had

A sample of water from Lake Nyos

A man stands near animals that were killed by the deadly gas in the air.

no time to act. The gas reached them too quickly. Without oxygen to breathe, people passed out and died within just a few minutes.

The cloud of gas kept rolling down the valley. It swept through three villages. The gas traveled 13 miles to the bottom of the valley. In all, the deadly gas killed 1,746 people. It also killed every other living **creature** in its path. As one man said, "Not even small ants could have survived."

Some villagers were not home at the time. So they survived. The next day many returned to see what had happened. It was a terrible sight. The gas did no harm to the buildings. But all the people were dead. Some were in bed. Others were at the dinner table. Still others were out in the streets. The gas killed them wherever it found them.

Still Dangerous

Lake Nyos no longer looked beautiful. The water that was left was all stirred up. It did not look clear blue. The whole lake had turned ugly shades of red and brown.

Even worse, the lake was still dangerous. Plenty of carbon dioxide remained on the bottom. So the lake could explode again at any moment. Because of this, no one was allowed to go back and live near the lake. **Survivors** had to leave their homes and move to refugee camps.

Lake Nyos is not the only lake in the world with carbon dioxide at the bottom. There are two others. Both are in Africa. One is Lake Monoun. The other is Lake Kivu.

Lake Kivu has never exploded. But Lake Monoun has. In 1984, carbon dioxide blew up out of it and killed 37 people. "These lakes are just **time bombs** waiting to go off," said scientist George Kling in 1999. "They could go off tomorrow."

Scientists like Kling are trying to solve the problem. One idea is to sink pipes down to the bottom of the lakes. The pipes could slowly pump out the gas. But such a plan would take huge amounts of time and money. So for now, people like Gambo Djibril and his family can only return to Lake Nyos in their dreams.

Read and Remember — Finish the Sentence

🐦 Circle the best ending for each sentence.

1. Before 1986, Lake Nyos looked _____.
   dirty   beautiful   tiny

2. Small amounts of carbon dioxide are put into _____.
   jet engines   eggs   soft drinks

3. Deadly gas was building up at the bottom of _____.
   Cameroon   Lake Nyos   Africa

4. On August 21, 1986, the lake _____.
   exploded   turned orange   became very cold

5. More than 1,700 people were killed by the _____.
   surprise storm   cloud of gas   terrible heat

Write About It

🐦 Imagine you are the son or daughter of Gambo Djibril. Write a paragraph describing what you miss about living near Lake Nyos.

_____

_____

_____

_____

_____

_____

_____

Focus on Vocabulary — Finish the Paragraphs

Use the words in dark print to complete the paragraphs. Reread the paragraphs to be sure they make sense.

disturbed	**carbon dioxide**	**refugee**	**volcanoes**
oxygen	**time bombs**	**survivors**	**craters**
crops	**creature**		

Lake Nyos sits near some old, quiet **(1)**_____ in Cameroon. The lake is in one of the hollow **(2)**_____. Until August 21, 1986, many people lived around Lake Nyos. They grew **(3)**_____ there. But on that August day, something **(4)**_____ the lake. Deadly gas from the bottom of the lake exploded into the air. This gas was **(5)**_____.

The gas was very strong and heavy. It pushed aside all the **(6)**_____, so people in the area could not breathe. The deadly gas killed every **(7)**_____ for miles around. The **(8)**_____ could no longer live near the dangerous lake. They had to move to **(9)**_____ camps.

There are two other lakes in the world which have deadly gas in them. Scientists say these lakes are **(10)**_____ that will someday explode.

Layers of a Lake

Deep lakes often have three layers of **temperature**. The sun warms the top layer of water. Fish and plants are most likely to live in this layer. The middle layer has few fish and plants. The bottom layer is very cold and has little or no light. Study the diagram below. Write the answer to each question.

Layers of a Lake

Top
Water is 65–75°F. Most fish live here.
There is plenty of food.

Middle
Water is 45–65°F.
Few fish live here.

Bottom
Water is 39–45°F. There is little light here.
Plants cannot grow. Only a few animals,
such as earthworms can live here.

1. What is the temperature range of the middle layer? _____

2. What is one kind of animal that can live in the bottom layer of the lake? _____

3. Which layer is the darkest layer? _____

4. Which layer is the warmest layer? _____

5. Why do most fish live in the top layer of the lake? _____

_____

Flooding Waters Bury Georgia

People in Georgia had never seen anything like it. On July 3, 1994, a strong storm moved into western Florida. It brought winds of more than 38 miles per hour. So it was labeled a **tropical storm** and given a name. It was called Tropical Storm Alberto. By July 4, the storm was hitting Georgia. But then it stopped moving. For several days Alberto stayed over Georgia. Winds from the storm blew fairly hard. But the real story of Alberto was the rain. Some places got 24 inches in one day. That was an inch of rain an hour! With so much rain, everyone knew floods would be a problem.

Rising Waters

By the night of July 4, rivers in Georgia began to **overflow**. Over the next five days, some rivers rose 20 feet above their **banks**. This meant more than a little flooding. It meant raging waters could sweep away cars and people.

One place that was hit hard was Albany. There the Flint River overflowed, flooding most of the town. Soon almost every building at Albany State College was underwater. The people of Albany were caught by surprise. Floods almost never hit their town.

Van Ditty had lived in Albany for 20 years. He said, "People in this area had little warning. Some people told me they woke up to the sound of frogs croaking and stepped out of their beds into two feet of water."

"They say we don't live in a **flood zone**," said Debbie Blanton of the Albany Red Cross. But this storm showed that if enough rain fell, any place could be flooded. Blanton's home was **destroyed** in the flood. The roaring waters even washed away her cars.

The Flint River flooded the town of Albany.

Bobby Arnold also lived in Albany. He, too, lost his home in the flood. Luckily, he and his family got out in time. They moved to a **shelter** on higher ground. "Our home is underwater," said Arnold. "We lost everything."

David Brantley was in even worse shape. He and his wife Pearlie Mae did not get out of their house in time. As water **swirled** into their home, the Brantleys ran up the stairs. They spent five frightening days in their dark attic.

By the fifth day, Pearlie Mae was so hungry she couldn't stand it any longer. She decided to go down to her flooded kitchen to search for food. She made it down the stairs. She even managed to climb onto the refrigerator. But then she slipped. She fell into the water and drowned. David Brantley was later found, weak but alive.

Car Trouble

Day after day the flooding continued. It knocked out bridges. It washed out roads. Cars and trucks stood little chance against the water's power. The raging waters tossed them around like toys. Trying to drive through Albany was very dangerous. The police put **barricades** up to keep cars out of flooded places.

In at least one case, the barricades didn't work. A driver from New Jersey didn't see them through the pounding rain. So he just kept driving. The man had six people with him. Two were small boys. As he drove, water washed up over the road. It swept the car into the river. The five adults were able to get out and swim to safety. The two small boys, however, didn't make it. They died in the rushing water.

In all, the flooding killed 28 Georgians. Most died in cars or trucks. With water rising quickly around them, the people inside tried to open the doors. But they couldn't. The doors were kept shut by the water. Soon water leaked in, so anyone trapped inside the cars and trucks drowned.

The rushing water washed out roads and knocked out bridges.

Cleaning Up

The governor of Georgia called the flood the worst **natural disaster** ever in the state. Others called it "the 500-year flood." By that, they meant such a bad flood happened only once every 500 years.

By July 9, the Flint River began to drop. Slowly, people went back to their homes. Bobby Arnold and others like him found nothing that could be saved. The rushing water had smashed furniture. Toys had been broken. Clothes had been ripped as they were swept out onto streets and lawns. The flood had also **polluted** the drinking water. It had washed dirt and garbage into people's wells. For days people had to drink bottled water.

Members of the National Guard and Red Cross hurried in to help. They cooked hot meals. They brought in clean water. They fixed telephone lines. John Lane even rescued a cat caught up in a tree. Then, just by luck, Lane found the 11-year-old girl who owned the cat. By working together, people were able to rebuild their lives. But it would be a long time before anyone in Albany forgot Tropical Storm Alberto.

The flood had ruined people's homes.

42

Read and Remember — Choose the Answer

Draw a circle around the correct answer.

1. What caused the flooding?

broken water pipes   too much rain   melting snow

2. Where did David Brantley go when his house flooded?

to a church   to a bank   to his attic

3. What was Pearlie Mae Brantley trying to get when she died?

blankets   food   her cat

4. Why did the driver from New Jersey drive past the barricades?

He didn't see them.   He was speeding.   He was late.

5. What did some people call the flood?

Alberto   the 500-year flood   the fast flood

Think About It — Fact or Opinion

A **fact** is a true statement. An **opinion** is a statement that tells what a person thinks. Write **F** beside each statement that is a fact. Write **O** beside each statement that is an opinion.

_____ **1.** Water spilled out of the Flint River.

_____ **2.** Rainy days are no fun.

_____ **3.** Most buildings at Albany State College flooded.

_____ **4.** Debbie Blanton picked a terrible place to live.

_____ **5.** The Brantleys should have gone someplace else.

_____ **6.** Twenty-eight Georgians died in the flooding.

_____ **7.** Georgia's governor didn't do enough to help people.

_____ **8.** After the flood, people were able to rebuild their lives.

Focus on Vocabulary — Finish Up

Choose the correct word in dark print to complete each sentence.

shelter	**polluted**	**natural disaster**	**destroyed**
overflow	**barricades**	**tropical storm**	**swirled**
banks	**flood zone**		

1. A storm with very high winds and much rain is called a

_____.

2. A place that covers or protects you is a _____.

3. To flow up over the top edge of something is to

_____.

4. When something is completely ruined, it is _____.

5. The rising ground along the sides of a river are its

_____.

6. To have spread harmful materials is to have _____.

7. A terrible event caused by nature is a _____.

8. If something spun around and around, it _____.

9. Fences put up to block the way are called _____.

10. An area in danger of being flooded is a _____.

Weather Map

A **weather map** shows what kind of weather to expect in an area. The map below shows one day's weather in the United States, Canada, and Mexico. The **map key** explains what the symbols or colors on the map mean. Study the map. Circle the answer to each question.

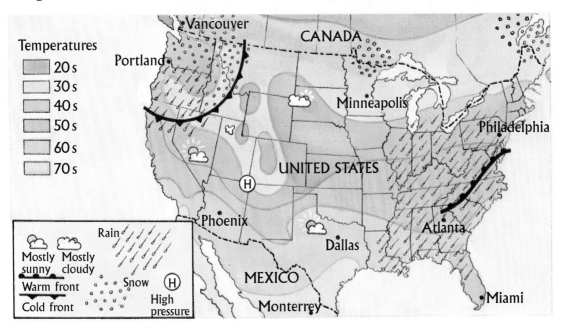

1. Which is the symbol for rain?

2. What is the weather like in Atlanta?

mostly sunny   rainy   snowy

3. Which city should expect a day that is mostly sunny?

Dallas   Portland   Philadelphia

4. Which city has about the same temperature as Dallas?

Phoenix   Miami   Vancouver

5. Which city has the coldest temperature?

Minneapolis   Philadelphia   Monterrey

Juba River Flood

ohamed Abdirisak stood on a hill in the African country of Somalia. He looked out across the Juba River Valley. This was where he lived. Usually he could see green fields dotted with houses, bridges, and roads. But in November 1997, Abdirisak saw a very different sight. The whole valley was filled with swirling brown water. His neighbors' houses were all gone. His own house, too, had disappeared under the raging water.

Too Much Rain

Abdirisak could barely believe his country's bad luck. In the early 1990s, Somalia needed rain. But the rain didn't come. The country lived through a terrible **drought**. Crops dried up. The land turned dusty and brown. People went hungry. Some even starved to death.

So Somalians were very happy when it began to rain in October 1997. They thought that this was one year they wouldn't have to worry about water. But the Somalians were wrong. Instead of getting light fall showers, East Africa got day after day of very heavy rain.

By the end of October, the **rainfall** in Somalia measured between 5 and 25 times the normal amount. The Juba River was no longer a slow, peaceful stream. It had become a dangerous, rushing **torrent**. Water rose to the top of the Juba River's banks. Then, as the rain continued, water spilled out across the valley.

The flooding in Somalia destroyed crops in the fields. It swept cows, camels, and people off their feet. It washed away thousands of homes. One of them was the house where Abdirisak lived. Water was everywhere.

No Way Out

In some places, the flood in Somalia grew to be eight miles wide. Eighty-five different villages became flooded. In many of these places, the people had no way to get out. Water had washed out all the roads. It had carried away bridges and covered airport runways.

With water roaring all around them, some people ran for patches of high ground. Other people **scrambled** up into trees. Still, others climbed onto rooftops. Mohamed Abdirisak ended up on a hill without food or shelter. He knew he would have to stay there until a boat or helicopter came.

People made boats out of anything they could.

Hippos threatened people who came near them.

Hippos threatened people who came near them.

All along the Juba River Valley, thousands of others also were waiting to be rescued. The long wait was hard for everyone. As the days dragged by, some people found that the **floodwater** was not their biggest problem. For them, the greatest danger came from wild animals.

Danger All Around

Like humans, these animals were disturbed by the flooding. As the rain continued to fall, the floodwaters covered more land. Soon crocodiles lost their normal resting places. They had to fight humans for what little dry ground was left. In one spot, an angry crocodile killed a man.

Hippos also were stirred up. They **threatened** anyone who came near them. **Poisonous** snakes swam through the water. Some of Abdirisak's neighbors killed a 13-foot snake that was headed their way.

Hyenas could not find their usual food. They **prowled** the edges of dry ground, growing hungrier and hungrier. Soon they were ready to kill and eat any human they could find.

By the middle of November, rain was still falling in Somalia. Over 230 square miles of crops and farmland were underwater. That was an area about the size of a large city. More than a thousand people had drowned. About 14,000 farm animals also had died.

Beyond that, the terrible flood had left 200,000 people without homes. Refugee camps were set up for them. But there wasn't enough food or clean water to go around. So many survivors became weak and sick.

In time, the rain finally did stop. But by then, Somalia was in **ruins**. It would take many months before people like Mohamed Abdirisak could return to a normal life.

The flood had left 200,000 people without food.

Read and Remember — Check the Events

Place a check in front of the three sentences that tell what happened in the story.

_____ **1.** Mohamed Abdirisak pulled his neighbors out of the mud.

_____ **2.** In the early 1990s, Somalia did not get enough rain.

_____ **3.** In the fall of 1997, Somalia got too much rain.

_____ **4.** People learned to live on houseboats in the river.

_____ **5.** Every wild animal near the Juba River died.

_____ **6.** People had to watch out for snakes, hippos, and crocodiles.

Write About It

Imagine you lived through the Juba River Flood. Write a letter to a friend, describing what you went through.

Dear _____ ,

_____

_____

_____

_____

_____

_____

_____

_____

USE WHAT YOU KNOW

Focus on Vocabulary — Crossword Puzzle

Use the clues to complete the puzzle. Choose from the words in dark print.

scrambled   hyenas   poisonous   ruins   torrent

floodwater   drought   threatened   prowled   rainfall

Across

3. water brought by floods

6. what is left after something has been smashed

7. flesh-eating mammals that live in Africa

8. a fast-rushing stream of water

9. moved quickly

Down

1. moved quietly like a wild animal

2. a long time without rain

4. gave signs of danger

5. able to cause sickness

6. the amount of rain that falls

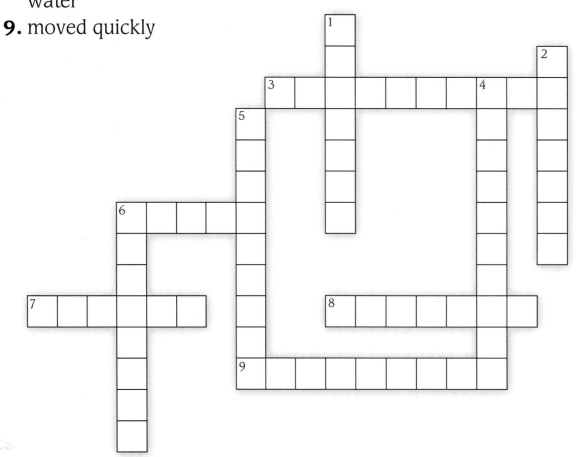

52

SCIENCE CONNECTION

Water Cycle

Water moves from Earth to the air and then back again. This movement is called the **water cycle**. First heat from the sun changes water to **water vapor**. The water vapor in the air forms clouds as it cools. Then these clouds return water to Earth as rain or snow. Study the diagram. Write the answer to each question.

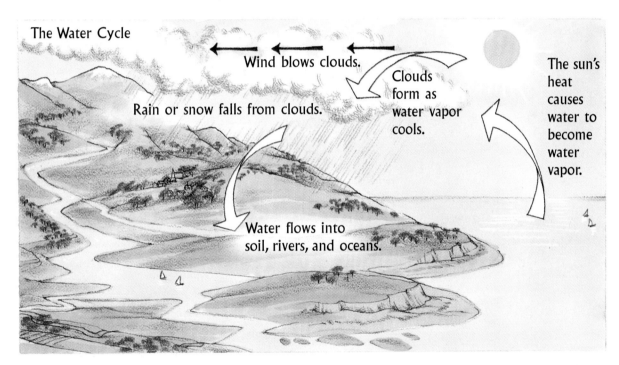

The Water Cycle

Wind blows clouds.

Clouds form as water vapor cools.

The sun's heat causes water to become water vapor.

Rain or snow falls from clouds.

Water flows into soil, rivers, and oceans.

1. What causes Earth's water to change to water vapor? _____

_____

2. What does water vapor form as it cools? _____

3. What moves clouds over the ocean to areas over land? _____

4. Where does water flow after it falls to Earth? _____

_____

5. How do clouds return water to Earth? _____

_____

53

A Dangerous Sport

Bob Tooker knew the Illinois River was dangerous. As it passes through Oregon, it has 36 miles of rapids. The water hits sharp rocks. It tumbles over waterfalls. All the splashing makes the water look white. This river is not the place for beginning **rafters**.

Bob Tooker was not a beginner. He had been rafting down rivers with **white water** for 18 years. But on March 21, 1998, he found out that even a good rafter can get in trouble on the Illinois River.

Good Days and Bad Days

Tooker had been down the Illinois River twice before. He knew it was a **challenge**. He said it was hard "even on a good day." A good day was one when the water level wasn't too high. On that kind of day, about 2,000 **cubic feet** of water flows through the river each second. That's enough to make rafting down the Illinois River thrilling but not deadly.

March 21 started out looking like a good day. The water level was not too high. Tooker knew that could change. Rain could **increase** the flow of water. So could melting snow from nearby mountains. But no heavy rain was expected. So Tooker thought the river would be safe.

Tooker and four friends put on their helmets. They slipped on their life jackets. Then they climbed into two large rubber rafts. The group was ready to go.

At first the trip went smoothly. But that afternoon it began to rain hard. Tooker and the others stopped

White water can toss rafts around.

rafting. As night came, they set up camp at the edge of the river. Then they tried to get some sleep.

The next morning they got up early. The heavy rain had raised the water level of the river. Melting snow from the mountains had made it even worse. The **volume** of water flowing downstream was now much higher than normal. In fact, it was five times higher than when Tooker and his friends had begun rafting.

Tooker knew they had to hurry. The river was still rising. As the flow increased, so would the danger. Rushing water could tip over their rafts. It could throw them against deadly rocks. The five men didn't even stop to eat breakfast. They just jumped into their rafts and headed downstream.

The Green Wall

Ahead of them was a deep **gorge**. This was a place where the river ran between two walls of rock.

The walls were very high. They went up 1,800 feet. That made them taller than any building in the world. This part of the river was called the Green Wall. The name came from the green **moss** that grew on the high walls.

The Green Wall was the **point of no return**. Once the rafters got there, they would have to keep going. They couldn't leave the river and climb onto dry ground. The walls of the gorge were simply too high.

As Tooker and his friends reached the Green Wall, the river was raging. The amount of water flowing through it was now 10 times greater than when they had started.

Within seconds, the roaring water flipped the rafts. All five men were dumped into the river. For the next mile, Tooker was swept along through the rapids. At last he managed to grab onto a rock near the edge of the river. He pulled himself up onto it.

Three of his friends did the same. Like Tooker, they were scared but alive. One friend, however, never made it onto a rock. Vern Byars drowned in rushing waters at the Green Wall.

Within seconds, roaring white water can flip rafts.

Helicopters flew in to rescue the stranded men.

Waiting to be Rescued

For hours, Tooker and his friends stayed on their rocks. They were not the only ones in trouble. There were 25 other people on the Illinois River that day. Some made it out safely. But one of the 25 drowned. Six others were **stranded** in the river. They were hanging onto rocks or trees along the edge of the rapids. Like Tooker and his friends, they were wet, cold, and frightened. They could only hope someone would come rescue them.

There was too much fog for any rescue effort to be made that day. But the next morning, the fog finally lifted. Helicopters flew in over the gorge. The pilots were taking a great risk. The gorge was so narrow that the helicopters barely fit between the walls. Still, the pilots managed to drop long wires down to the water. One by one, all ten people stranded there were pulled up.

Bob Tooker was happy to be rescued. But he felt terrible about his friend's death. "It'll be a long time before I sort it all out," he said. "Will I ever get back in a boat again? I don't know."

Read and Remember — Finish the Sentence

Circle the best ending for each sentence.

1. Tooker and his friends all wore _____.
parachutes   helmets   safety ropes

2. While Tooker was rafting, it began to _____.
snow   rain   get hot

3. That night the group camped _____.
at the river's edge   on a mountain   in a parking lot

4. Tooker's raft flipped when he reached the _____.
Illinois Rock   Dead Man's Pass   Green Wall

5. Ten rafters were rescued by _____.
divers   helicopters   a small boat

Think About It — Drawing Conclusions

Write one or more sentences to answer each question.

1. Why do people go rafting on the Illinois River? _____

_____

2. What made the level of the river rise so much? _____

_____

3. Why didn't the men stop to eat breakfast the next morning?

_____

4. Why did Tooker and his friends stay on their rocks for hours?

_____

_____

USE WHAT YOU KNOW

Focus on Vocabulary — Match Up

Match each word with its meaning. Darken the circle beside the correct answer.

1. rafters

    ○ workers   ○ pilots   ○ people who ride rafts

2. white water

    ○ rough, foamy water   ○ water with fish   ○ salty water

3. volume

    ○ tall, thin line   ○ amount   ○ full of hard rocks

4. moss

    ○ soft green plant   ○ kind of tree   ○ a flowering bush

5. cubic feet

    ○ puddles   ○ units for measuring water   ○ wind speed

6. stranded

    ○ pulled up   ○ moved to a new place   ○ stuck

7. increase

    ○ divide into parts   ○ make bigger   ○ leave behind

8. point of no return

    ○ start   ○ place where one can't turn back   ○ time

9. gorge

    ○ place with high walls   ○ deep river   ○ heavy rain

10. challenge

    ○ hard work   ○ change of plans   ○ decision

The Age of a River

Rivers change over time. When rivers are young, they move very fast and have slanted **slopes**. They often have many **rapids** and **waterfalls**. Over time, the water running in the rivers wears away the land. Then the rivers' slopes become flat. Older rivers have no rapids or waterfalls. The pictures below show four different rivers. Write **A**, **B**, **C**, or **D** to answer the questions.

1. Which river has a waterfall? _____

2. Which river is winding? _____

3. Does River B or River D have a flat slope? _____

4. Which two rivers are young rivers? _____

5. Which two rivers are old rivers? _____

Trouble on the Beach

Raymond Nimis was looking forward to a quiet evening. He planned to spend it at home with his wife and baby daughter. Nimis lived in Arop. That was a small village on the north coast of Papua New Guinea. Like everyone else in the village, Nimis lived right near the Pacific Ocean. He was used to the sound of waves hitting the beach. But at 7:30 P.M. on July 17, 1998, the ocean began to make a very different sound. It started to roar like a jet engine.

Three Giant Waves

The roar came from three huge waves that were headed for shore. Twenty minutes earlier, a strong earthquake had occurred far out to sea. The ground under the water shook. That caused a tsunami. Now three huge waves were headed straight for Papua New Guinea. The waves were **separated** by many miles. But they were traveling hundreds of miles an hour. They were going as fast as a speeding race car. So they would hit land just a few minutes apart.

Each of these waves was about 18 miles long. The biggest one was close to 30 feet high. That made it as tall as a telephone pole.

Some people saw the tsunami coming. "I was right there in the village next to the **coastline**," said Paul Saroya. "We saw the sea rising up and then it started moving toward the village." Saroya and his family ran as fast as possible away from the beach.

Clara Asupot saw the first big wave coming. She was in a nearby village. Asupot had never seen anything like it before. She knew she had to move quickly to save herself and her two small sons. She picked up her children. Then she jumped into a nearby canoe. She hoped that she and her sons could ride the giant wave to safety.

The Tsunami Strikes

As the tsunami neared, Raymond Nimis felt his house shake. The house was made of bark and leaves from the nearby **jungle**. It was not very strong. Still, it was built for the beach. The house stood on top of long wooden poles called **stilts**. Ocean waves could wash right under the house without hurting it.

This wave, however, was far too big to fit under Nimis's house. "The wave crashed onto the house," he said. The **force** of the wave destroyed the roof and walls. Nimis's wife and daughter disappeared in a rush of water.

Nimis grabbed a piece of wood. He hung onto it as the wave carried him into the air. He saw friends and neighbors wash past in a **blur**. Many were screaming and crying. Others were already dead. "People were dying everywhere," he said.

An earthquake far below the ocean had caused the giant waves.

Clara Asupot sat in the canoe holding her sons. The first wave swept the canoe off the ground. It carried Asupot and her sons into the jungle. The canoe was so far off the ground that it got stuck in the branches of a tree. That's where Asupot and her children stayed until the tsunami died down.

Some people tried to run away from the huge waves. Others climbed trees. Some made it to safety. Paul Saroya and his family escaped harm. But sadly, thousands of others did not. Most small children couldn't run fast enough to get away. They were too little to climb trees. So they drowned in the waves of the **salt water**. "So many babies were lost," said one woman.

Pain and Fear

As the last giant wave died away, Raymond Nimis was still holding on to a piece of wood. He looked around in **horror**. His entire village was gone. Every home had been washed away. Many of his neighbors were dead. His wife and daughter were lost forever.

Raymond Nimis was not badly hurt. But many other survivors were. Some people had been hit by floating trees. They had broken bones and deep cuts. Some people had been washed out into the sea. They had spent hours holding on to pieces of wood. Water had gotten into their **lungs**. Their cuts and scrapes were **infected**.

After the tsunami, Clara Asupot wanted to get far away from the water. So she took her children high up into the mountains behind the beach. That's where many survivors went. They built small shelters there. They ate coconuts, bananas, and whatever else they could find growing in the jungle.

At night, the mountain air was cold. No one had warm clothing to wear. Asupot worried that her children would get sick. But she was too frightened to return to the beach. Asupot and many others would make the mountains their new home. They wanted to be far away from the beach. To them, the ocean would never seem safe again.

A young survivor looks out from the jungle.

Read and Remember — Choose the Answer

Draw a circle around the correct answer.

1. Where did Raymond Nimis and his neighbors live?

   in the mountains   near the ocean   in a deep valley

2. What did the tsunami sound like as it neared the village?

   a loud scream   a hammer   a jet engine

3. What did Clara Asupot do when she saw the wave coming?

   She went home.   She got in a canoe.   She hid.

4. What happened to Nimis's village?

   It was washed away.   It was buried.   It burned.

5. Where did Clara Asupot go after the tsunami?

   to a big city   into the mountains   to a hotel

Write About It

Imagine you are Raymond Nimis or Clara Asupot. Write a letter to a friend, describing how it feels to have survived a tsunami.

Dear _____ ,

_____

_____

_____

_____

_____

Focus on Vocabulary — Make a Word

Choose a word in dark print to complete each sentence. Write the letters of the word on the blanks. When you are finished, the letters in the circles will tell you what part of Papua New Guinea was hit by the tsunamis.

horror	infected	salt water	jungle	separated
blur	force	stilts	lungs	coastline

1. People gathered food from the _____.

     _ _ ◯ _ _

2. The _____ of the water washed away houses.

     _ _ ◯ _ _

3. Nimis saw people wash past him in a _____.

     _ _ _ ◯

4. Nimis's house stood on tall _____.

     _ _ ◯ _ _ _

5. Nimis looked around in _____ at what he saw.

     ◯ _ _ _ _ _

6. People's cuts and scrapes became _____.

     _ _ _ _ ◯ _ _ _

7. Many people lived right near the _____.

     _ ◯ _ _ _ _ _ _ _

8. The waves were _____ by many miles.

     _ _ _ _ ◯ _ _ _ _

9. Water got into some people's _____.

     _ _ _ _ ◯

10. Many children drowned in the _____.

     _ _ _ ◯ _ _ _ _ _

Wave Movement

Most waves start as long, wide **swells** at sea. As they near shore, they slow down and get higher. Finally, they fall. The falling waves are called **surf**. Then water flows back to the ocean as **backwash**. Study the wave diagram. Circle the answer that best completes each sentence.

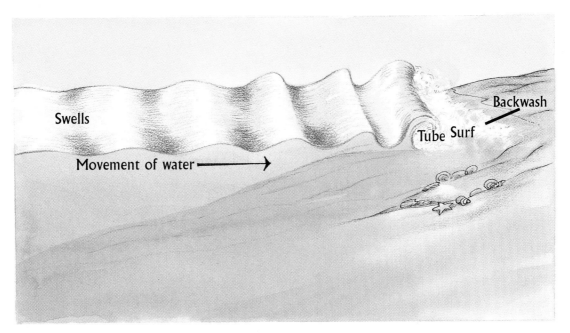

1. Swells are _____.
   long waves at sea   splashes of water   earthquakes

2. At shore, a wave _____.
   gets smaller   gets higher   speeds up

3. When waves fall, they are called _____.
   tubes   swells   surf

4. As a wave starts to fall, it might form a _____.
   backwash   surf   tube

5. Backwash is water that flows _____.
   back to the ocean   over buildings   back to the shore

Horror in the Philippines

It had been an awful year for the people of the Philippines. In 1998, one **rainstorm** after another hit this Asian country. Each storm brought high winds, heavy rains, and floods. Just when people **recovered** from one storm, another one hit. Rolando Castor wondered if the bad weather would ever end. Castor lived near the Philippines' Pampanga River. By October, he and his family of ten were tired of the rain. They hoped the worst was behind them. But in fact, the worst was yet to come.

Wind and Water

On October 22, 1998, the ninth big storm of the year struck the Philippines. It was called **Typhoon** Babs. A typhoon is a powerful rainstorm that builds over warm ocean water. It brings high winds and lots of rain. In the Atlantic Ocean this kind of storm is called a **hurricane**. In the western Pacific Ocean it is called a typhoon. Like a hurricane, a typhoon is labeled with a name.

Typhoon Babs began as a tiny ocean storm on October 14. Its top winds were only 25 miles per hour. But it quickly gained strength. When its winds reached 74 miles per hour, scientists began to measure the storm's power on a scale. The scale put the storm within a **category**. The categories range from one to five. One is the weakest and five is the strongest. By October 20, Typhoon Babs was a category five storm. It had top winds of 135 miles per hour. Weather expert Leny Ruiz warned, "This typhoon is going to be no joke."

The heavy floods destroyed houses, farms, and bridges.

Ruiz was right. Typhoon Babs blasted into the Philippines on October 22. It caused huge amounts of **damage**. High winds knocked down power lines. Thousands of coconut trees were blown over. The winds also ripped the roofs off houses.

Still, it was not the wind that did the most damage. It was the rain. The rain caused a lot of flooding. On one Philippine island, floods destroyed four out of every five houses. That left thousands of families without a place to stay. Floods swept over farms, destroying rice and other crops. Raging water knocked out bridges and washed out roads. High waters caused dams to break, adding to the flooding.

In the hills, the rain caused **landslides**. Dirt, mud, and trees washed down onto buildings and roads. These landslides killed many people. "It's like a war **zone**," said Orlando Mercado, a Philippine leader. "It's as if a bomb has been dropped."

Trying to Get Away

Rolando Castor and his family were among those who lost their home. The Pampanga River flooded so quickly that the Castor family barely got out in time. "We left when the water was suddenly up to here," said Rolando Castor, pointing to his neck. "We had no canoe. So the adults were carrying the children."

The Castor family made it to a small church. So did seven other families. They found the first floor under water. But the church had a second floor. So the Castors and the others crowded up into it. Here they waited for the flooding to end.

Other people from the area also tried to get away. They hurried along railroad tracks and roads leading to drier land. When night came, they set up camp along the tracks and roads. Some people used plastic sheets as tents. Many people just found a high patch of ground and **huddled** there, hoping the water would not reach them.

Some families stayed in their homes. But the rising water soon forced many of them onto their roofs. People brought chickens, pets, and even tables up onto the roof with them. They knew the flood would destroy whatever they left behind.

The rising water forced many people to get on their rooftops.

73

People stayed on their rooftops for days, waiting to be rescued. Others did not last that long. In some places, the water rose up and over the roofs. When that happened, entire families were washed away.

Hard Work Ahead

In all, Typhoon Babs killed nearly 200 people. It **affected** more than two million others. Families lost homes. Business owners lost stores and supplies. Farmers lost crops, fields, and farm buildings. Children found their schools had been destroyed.

But the Philippine people had been through typhoons before. They knew what they had to do to rebuild their country. Right away, people began building new homes. Those who had food shared with those who did not. Farmers started planting crops again. It would take many months before life returned to normal. But the people did not give up hope. "We are slowly doing it," one rescue worker said.

Read and Remember — Check the Events

Place a check in front of the three sentences that tell what happened in the story.

_____ **1.** High winds knocked down power lines and trees.

_____ **2.** The Pampanga River flooded.

_____ **3.** Rolando Castor was very worried when a church roof blew off.

_____ **4.** A plane was blown out of the sky.

_____ **5.** Water washed a train engine right off railroad tracks.

_____ **6.** Some Philippine people were stranded on their rooftops for days.

Think About It — Find the Main Ideas

Underline the two most important ideas from the story.

1. Typhoon Babs did a lot of damage in the Philippines.

2. A weather expert said that the storm would be "no joke."

3. The storm touched the lives of more than two million people.

4. The Castor family stayed in a two-story church.

5. Some people brought chickens onto the roof with them.

6. Typhoon Babs began as a tiny ocean storm.

Focus on Vocabulary — Find the Meaning

Read each sentence. Circle the best meaning for the word in dark print.

1. There was one **rainstorm** after another.

   great idea   snowstorm   storm with lots of rain

2. In October 1998, a **typhoon** hit the Philippines.

   big accident   powerful storm with rain   ship

3. The storm was rated a **category** five.

   level   number of days   area of land

4. The storm caused a lot of **damage**.

   worry   cheering   harm

5. The Atlantic Ocean is where a **hurricane** forms.

   wave   large ship   strong ocean storm

6. **Landslides** killed many people.

   soil sliding down hills   floods   shaking ground

7. People **huddled** along railroad tracks.

   moved quickly   got down   crowded together

8. The storm **affected** more than two million people.

   buried   had touched   surprised

9. The places the storm hit looked like a war **zone**.

   area of land   game   weapon

10. It was a long time before people **recovered** from the storm.

   remembered   got better   fled

Nature Can Prevent Floods

Heavy rains can cause flooding. But nature has ways to help prevent floods. High **banks** along rivers are called **levees**. Wide **channels** allow more water to move along the river. Trees keep soil in place along the banks. Study the diagram. Write the answer to each question.

Channels are the places where water in rivers usually flows.

Levees are high banks.

Tree roots hold soil in place.

1. What is a levee? _____

_____

2. What helps hold soil in place on the banks? _____

3. What is a channel? _____

_____

4. Would a wide channel or a narrow channel be less likely to have a flood? _____

5. If a bank becomes worn away by water, is a flood more or less likely to occur? _____

Survival at Sea

Isabel Arriola was a teacher. But she wasn't at school in late October 1998. Instead, Arriola was home with her husband and three children. She lived in a small fishing village in the Central American country of Honduras.

Arriola was waiting for the strong winds and rain of Hurricane Mitch to pass out of the area. But the hurricane had stopped moving. It **stalled** over Honduras. It brought more rain than Arriola had ever seen. All this rain would soon turn her life into a nightmare.

A River Overflows

By October 28, the river near Arriola's home could hold no more water. As the heavy rain kept coming, this river flooded its banks. Water rushed toward the Caribbean Sea, three miles away. Arriola's house stood between the river and the sea. So the **gushing** water headed straight for her home.

When the water reached Arriola's house, she and her family climbed onto the roof. Here the wind and rain **battered** them. But they **clung** to each other, hoping the floodwaters would soon die away.

That didn't happen. Instead, the swirling waters kept rising. Suddenly, the walls of the house caved in. Arriola felt herself falling into the cold, muddy water. Then she was swept away toward the open sea. The rest of her family disappeared in the raging water. Arriola would never see any of them again.

As she tumbled through the water, Arriola tried to keep her head up. "I tried to float so I could see over the water," Arriola later said. "I swam and swam...

trying to get somewhere dry. And then I realized I was already in the sea."

It was true. The floodwater had swept Arriola out into the Caribbean Sea. Through the rain, she could see branches of trees that had been carried out to sea with her. She could see boards and bits of metal. She could also see the bodies of dead cows and pigs.

Hanging On

For the next three hours, Arriola splashed and kicked to keep from drowning. She could feel herself growing tired. But there was no land in sight. At last she pulled herself up onto a **clump** of tree roots that was floating by. The wind and waves kept knocking her off. But again and again she climbed back on.

Each time she was knocked off, Arriola swallowed more salt water. That made her sick to her stomach. It also made her very thirsty. In addition, the high waves made her **seasick**. But Arriola did not give up.

The rains from Hurricane Mitch caused terrible floods.

Hours passed. Soon whole days and nights went by. Yet Arriola still clung to those tree roots.

"I cried every day," she later said. "I was crying more than I was quiet. Day and night I cried and screamed." Arriola tried to keep her mind on other things. Sometimes she still cried but other times she sang. From time to time, she even talked out loud to herself. At one point, she spotted a duck swimming in the water. "I talked for a long time to that duck, as if I were talking to a person," she said. "When it flew away, I felt so sad, so alone."

Too Much Water, Too Much Sun

Now and then Arriola saw coconuts and oranges floating in the water. She also saw grapefruit and pineapples. She grabbed as many as she could. She ate them to fight off her terrible thirst.

At last the rain stopped. But that brought a new problem. Arriola began to get sunburned. She took

81

turns lying on her back, stomach, and sides. That way she hoped not to get too badly burned. Still, the skin on her legs was soon peeling off. Meanwhile, her toes had been in the water so long that **fungus** had begun growing on them.

By November 3, Arriola was eighty miles north of Honduras. She had been drifting for six days and nights. During this time, she had not gotten enough to drink. So she was very **dehydrated**. Also, she had **hypothermia**. That meant her body temperature was dropping too low. She could not stay warm with the cool water splashing over her all the time. If she got much colder, she would die.

Finally, Arriola saw an airplane flying overhead. She grabbed a red cup that was floating by. Then she waved it weakly, hoping the pilot would see her.

The pilot did see her. An hour later, a helicopter arrived and pulled Arriola safely out of the water. She had been through a terrible **ordeal**. But she had survived.

Arriola had survived a terrible ordeal.

Read and Remember — Finish the Sentence

Circle the best ending for each sentence.

1. Arriola and her family climbed onto _____.

the roof   a fence   a car

2. Arriola was swept out into the sea by _____.

floodwaters   tornado   waterfall

3. Arriola felt sick from swallowing _____.

rotten fruit   seaweed   salt water

4. At one point, Arriola talked to a _____.

dog   duck   grapefruit

5. Arriola's legs became _____.

sunburned   bloody   covered with cuts

Write About It

Imagine you are a newspaper reporter. Write three questions that you would like to ask Isabel Arriola.

1. _____

_____

2. _____

_____

3. _____

_____

Focus on Vocabulary — Crossword Puzzle

Use the clues to complete the puzzle. Choose from the words in dark print.

ordeal   **gushing**   **battered**   **clung**   **clump**

seasick   **dehydrated**   **hypothermia**   **stalled**   **fungus**

Across

1. feeling ill from the motion of waves
5. something that grows in wet places
7. without enough water
8. hung on tight
9. a dangerously low body temperature

Down

2. stopped moving
3. pouring out
4. hit again and again
6. painful or terrible experience
8. group or cluster

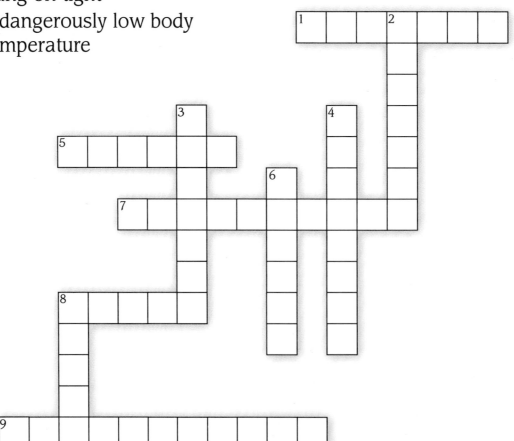

How Rain Forms

How do rain and clouds form? First the sun causes water to **evaporate** and form **water vapor**. As the water vapor rises and cools, it turns into tiny water droplets. These droplets form clouds and rain. Study the diagram below. Write **1**, **2**, **3**, **4**, and **5** to show the correct order. The first one is done for you.

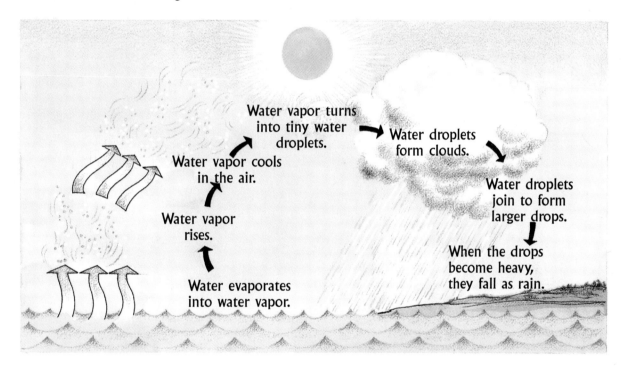

_____ Water vapor cools into water droplets.

_____ Clouds form.

___**1**___ Water evaporates into water vapor.

_____ Heavy drops fall as rain.

_____ Water droplets join to form larger drops.

Disaster in Australia

It looked like great weather for sailing. The sun was out and there was a good wind. On December 26, 1998, 115 **yachts** left Sydney, Australia. They were racing toward Hobart on the island of Tasmania.

The race from Sydney to Hobart had been held every year for 54 years. The race ran through the Tasman Sea past the Bass **Strait**. It covered 725 miles. The crews knew the water could be rough. That was part of the excitement. But this year's race would be more than exciting. It would be deadly.

Bad Weather Ahead

As the yachts took off, people knew the good weather would not last. A **gale** was expected. That meant winds blowing between 32 and 63 miles per hour. Such winds would kick up big waves. Still, the crews on the yachts were not worried. They thought they could handle any ocean storm that came their way.

Within 24 hours, they realized they were wrong. The ships ran into a small but very strong **windstorm**. The winds in this storm were like the powerful winds of a hurricane. That meant they were blowing more than 74 miles per hour.

Sayonara, an 80-foot yacht, was leading the way. It hit the storm first. The *Sayonara's* crew felt the wind roar past them at 90 miles per hour. The waves were as high as a four-story building. These waves bounced the *Sayonara* around like a toy. Crew members held on tight to keep from being washed **overboard**.

The crew of the *Sayonara* had looked foward to the race.

The *Sayonara* made it through the storm. But other ships were not so lucky. Those farther back caught the worst waves. One of those yachts was the *Winston Churchill*.

The *Churchill* had been around a long time. It had sailed in the first Sydney to Hobart race back in 1945. Since then, it had entered the race 17 more times. It had also sailed around the world. So the yacht had survived many rough seas. But it had never been in a storm like this before.

The End of an Old Ship

For hours, wind and waves blasted the *Churchill*. The nine crew members had to crawl on their hands and knees to get around on the ship. "You couldn't stand up," said crew member Paul Lumpton. "If you stood up, you would be thrown down."

Then a **rogue wave** hit the *Churchill*. A rogue wave is a single wave that is much bigger than those around it. This one was 80 feet high. It was so high and so **steep** that the *Churchill* couldn't make it over the top. The yacht went partway up the wave then fell back down. It was like climbing a wall but falling off before getting all the way up. The ship fell 30 feet straight down into the water below.

Lumpton and the other crew members survived the fall. But the ship did not. It began to fill with water. Five of the men jumped into one life raft. Lumpton and the three others jumped into another raft. They clung to these rafts as the *Winston Churchill* sank to the bottom of the sea.

Hour after hour, the two rafts were slammed around by the storm. They were washed far away from each other. Said Paul Lumpton, "Every time a wave would come, I could just see the **terror** in everybody's face." Lumpton's raft was badly battered by the waves. But the other raft was in even worse shape. It soon began to fall apart.

Death at Sea

John Stanley was one of the men who was in the raft that fell apart. He grabbed a piece of the raft and hung on tight. The four men with him tried hard to do the same. But the sea was terribly rough. Three of the four men lost their grip.

The *Winston Churchill* sank after it was hit by a rogue wave.

Stanley saw these men being washed away. For a while, he could see their heads bobbing up and down. "Boys," he thought to himself, "I hope you can hang in there until **daybreak**." But they couldn't. Sometime during the night, the three men drowned.

Meanwhile, rescue workers were trying to save the lives of people caught in the storm. Helicopter crews made amazing rescues. They pulled more than 50 sailors to safety. Rescue workers picked up John Stanley. They also saved the men on Paul Lumpton's raft. "When we heard that helicopter coming, we all had tears in our eyes," Lumpton said.

In the end, the *Sayonara* won the race. But few people cared. The natural disaster that hit the race made surviving much more important than winning. During the race, a total of six sailors drowned. Six ships sank or had to be **abandoned**. Only 39 boats got to Hobart. The rest stopped in harbors along the way. Many sailors agreed with the *Sayonara's* captain, Larry Ellison. Ellison said that if he lived to be 1,000 years old, he didn't think he would ever enter this race again.

A member of the crew from the *Winston Churchill* was safe at last.

Read and Remember — Choose the Answer

📖 **Draw a circle around the correct answer.**

1. Where did the race begin?

Sydney   Honduras   Hobart

2. What did the ship have to sail through?

heavy snow   muddy water   high waves

3. What happened to the *Winston Churchill*?

It sank.   It burned.   It hit another ship.

4. What did Paul Lumpton climb into?

a barrel   a life raft   a small fishing boat

5. Which yacht won the race?

the *Winston Churchill*   the *Hobart*   the *Sayonara*

Think About It — Find the Sequence

📖 **Number the sentences to show the correct order from the story. The first one is done for you.**

_____ **1.** John Stanley grabbed a part of the life raft and held on tight.

__1__ **2.** The *Sayonara* left Sydney.

_____ **3.** Rescue workers picked up Paul Lumpton.

_____ **4.** The *Winston Churchill's* crew crawled on their hands and knees.

_____ **5.** A rogue wave hit the *Winston Churchill*.

Focus on Vocabulary — Finish Up

Choose the correct word or words in dark print to complete each sentence.

yachts	**abandoned**	**strait**	**overboard**	**rogue wave**
terror	**windstorm**	**gale**	**daybreak**	**steep**

1. A feeling of great fear is _____.

2. Ships used for pleasure trips are _____.

3. Something that goes up sharply is _____.

4. A _____ is a wind that blows between 32 and 63 miles per hour.

5. A small strip of water that joins two larger bodies of water is a _____.

6. Something that has been left behind forever has been _____.

7. The time in the morning when light first appears is _____.

8. A storm with high winds is a _____.

9. If something falls over the side of a ship, it has fallen _____.

10. A wave much bigger than the waves around it is a _____.

SCIENCE CONNECTION

Wind and Waves

As wind moves across water, it causes larger waves to form. It is the wave's **energy**, not the water, that moves from wave to wave. Study the diagram below. Circle the best answer to each question.

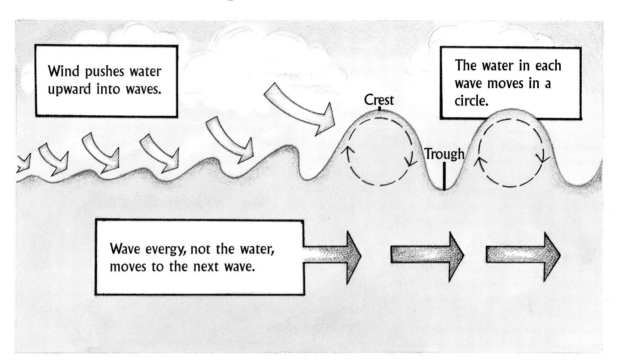

Wind pushes water upward into waves.

The water in each wave moves in a circle.

Crest

Trough

Wave evergy, not the water, moves to the next wave.

1. What is formed as wind moves across the water?
   larger waves   smaller waves   smooth water

2. What is the top of a wave called?
   energy   water circle   crest

3. What is the bottom of a wave called?
   trough   crest   undertow

4. What travels from wave to wave?
   crest   water   energy

5. How does water in a wave move?
   in a circle   from one crest to another   very slowly

A Dark Wall of Water

Tammi Levine had never been **canyoning** before. But it sounded exciting. People told her that canyoning was a mix of hiking, rock climbing, and swimming in white water. Levine was on vacation in Switzerland. In three days, she would be flying home to Maryland. She wanted to do one more exciting thing before she left. So on July 27, 1999, she signed up to go canyoning. It was a decision she would later **regret**.

Getting Ready

That afternoon, Levine got ready to go. Forty-four other people did the same thing. A company called Adventure World was in charge of the trip. The company sent eight **guides** to lead the group. Before heading out, the guides made sure everyone was wearing a **wet suit**. They also gave everyone helmets and life jackets.

The plan was to hike down into the Saxeten River Gorge near the town of Interlaken. At the bottom, the group would climb into the water. Then they would swim downstream toward Lake Brienz.

Along the way, they would climb over wet rocks. They would slide through rapids. They would even jump feet first over waterfalls. If a waterfall looked too big, they would use ropes to lower themselves over it.

At 4:30 P.M. the group set out. By then, dark clouds filled the sky. A fire **official** named Michael Seemater saw them leave. He tried to stop them. Seemater warned the guides that a rainstorm was coming. That could mean trouble down in the gorge. Heavy rains could cause a **flash flood**. Water levels would rise quickly in the narrow **canyon**. There would be no way for swimmers to climb to safety. But the guides didn't listen to Seemater's warnings. "We know what we're doing," one guide told Seemater.

A Wall of Water

As the group began hiking down into the gorge, rain did start to fall. "It was raining a little bit, but nothing bad," said Levine. Besides, the sky soon cleared. So she didn't think any more about it. She didn't realize that the storm had dumped a lot of water farther **upstream**.

At the bottom of the gorge, Levine and the others began splashing down the Saxeten River. They had no idea a flash flood was heading toward them.

Canyoning is a mix of hiking, rock climbing, and swimming in white water.

Tammy Levine will never forget the dangerous flash flood.

"The water looked clear and blue," Levine later said. "Then, all of a sudden, there was a muddy, dirty black wall of water. We had no warning. Suddenly, it was there, taking everything with it...."

Some people ahead of Levine were standing on a big rock when the wall of water rushed through. "One of them grabbed me and pulled me to the top," said Levine. "I was just shaking. I was crying. Everyone was trying to calm me down, telling me to **relax**. But I couldn't. I was scared to death."

Levine had a right to be scared. The huge wave of water was terribly strong. It carried mud, branches, and even tree trunks with it. The water crashed against the walls of the gorge with great force. It ripped the clothing off some of the people stranded there. It carried some of them away.

John Hall was one who was swept away by the rushing water. He was thrown against rocks and the walls of the gorge. Much of the time, his head was underwater. He tried to reach out and grab some of the bushes growing on the walls of the gorge. But it was impossible. The water kept pushing him downstream. At last, Hall made it to the end of the gorge. "Suddenly, I was in calmer water and safe," he said. Others were not so lucky. Many of them drowned or were smashed to death against the rocks.

The Terrible Truth

Meanwhile, Tammi Levine still clung to her rock. "After about 45 minutes, the water slowed down a little," she said. "We were able to get off the rock and onto land." By then, Levine was very tired. "I was so weak," she said. "I couldn't walk anymore. Other people were helping me."

Although Levine was worn out, she felt the worst was over. But she was wrong. The worst part was learning what had happened to others in the gorge. Levine thought everyone had made it out safely. "I thought everyone was on a rock like me," she said. Then officials told her the truth. Twenty-one people had died in the flash flood. It took rescue workers days to find all the bodies.

After the **tragedy**, Levine just wanted to go home. "You don't ever believe that something like this is going to happen to you," she said. "I think I'll cry about it for a long time."

Rescue workers search for survivors of the flash flood.

Read and Remember — Check the Events

Place a check in front of the three sentences that tell what happened in the story.

_____ **1.** Tammi Levine decided to go canyoning.

_____ **2.** Levine's group tried to climb some tall trees.

_____ **3.** John Hall was swept up by rushing water.

_____ **4.** Twenty-one people died in the Saxeten River Gorge.

_____ **5.** Tammi Levine was dragged a mile through the water.

_____ **6.** It took rescue workers five days to reach Levine.

Write About It

Imagine you are Tammi Levine. Write a letter to a friend, describing what happened to you in the Saxeten River Gorge.

Dear _____,

_____

_____

_____

_____

_____

_____

_____

_____

Focus on Vocabulary — Finish the Paragraphs

Use the words in dark print to complete the paragraphs. Reread the paragraphs to be sure they make sense.

wet suit	**flash flood**	**guides**	**upstream**	**regret**
canyoning	**tragedy**	**official**	**canyon**	**relax**

On July 27, 1999, Tammi Levine went **(1)**_____. She put on a **(2)**_____. Then she and 43 others followed eight **(3)**_____ down into a narrow **(4)**_____. An **(5)**_____ warned the group that a storm was coming. But the group went anyway. They would later **(6)**_____ not listening to the warning.

The group thought there wouldn't be a storm because only a little rain fell. But the storm had dumped a lot of water farther **(7)**_____. The group did not know this. Then they became caught in a **(8)**_____. Rushing water flowed through the canyon. The people in the group tried to hold on to anyone or anything. Levine was lucky. Some people grabbed her and pulled her onto a big rock in the middle of the river. They told Levine to **(9)**_____. But she had a right to be scared. Twenty-one people in the river drowned. The trip had turned into a **(10)**_____ for everyone.

Water Effects

Fast-moving water in rivers **erodes**, or wears away, the land or **banks** of rivers by carrying away rocks and soil. This moving water can form **canyons**, **gorges**, valleys, and **waterfalls**. As a river slows down, soil and rocks settle. This can change the path of a river and can form **deltas**. Study the diagram. Write the answer to each question.

Fast-moving water can wear away a river's bed to form a deep canyon or gorge.

Rapids and waterfalls form where land is steep.

A slow, winding river can form a wide valley.

Deltas form when soil collects at the mouth of a slow-moving river.

1. How is a gorge formed? _____

_____

2. Where do rapids occur? _____

3. What can a winding river form? _____

4. Where does a delta form? _____

5. What does fast-moving water wear away? _____

GLOSSARY

Words with this symbol can be found in the SCIENCE CONNECTION.

abandoned   page 90
Abandoned means left behind.

affected   page 74
Affected means touched or struck in some way.

backwash   page 69
Backwash is the water that flows back to the ocean.

banks   pages 39, 77, 101
Banks are the higher ground at the edges of rivers, streams, or lakes.

barricades   page 41
Barricades are fences set up to close a road.

battered   page 79
Battered means hit again and again.

bay   page 7
A bay is an area of water that is partly surrounded by land.

blur   page 64
A blur is something that has a hazy outline and is hard to see.

canyon   pages 96, 101
A canyon is a deep valley with tall sides.

canyoning   page 95
Canyoning is a mix of hiking, rock climbing, and white-water swimming.

carbon dioxide   page 31
Carbon dioxide is a heavy, colorless, odorless gas that does not burn.

category   page 71
A category is a class or level.

challenge   page 55
A challenge is hard work. It can require all of a person's skills.

channels   page 77
Channels are the deep part of a river.

cliff   page 23
A cliff is a high, steep wall of rock or ice.

clump   page 80
A clump is a group of things bunched together.

clung   page 79
Clung means held on tightly.

coastline   page 63
A coastline is the line where land meets the sea.

container   page 17
A container is something such as a bottle or a box.

craters   page 31
Craters are hollow areas in the ground or in volcanoes.

creature   page 33
A creature is a living being.

crest   page 26
A crest is the top of something such as a wave.

crops   page 31
Crops are plants, such as corn, that can be grown and gathered.

cubic feet   page 55
Cubic feet are units of measure. One cubic foot of water equals 7.481 gallons.

current   pages 16, 29
A current is water moving in a certain direction.

damage   page 72
Damage is harm caused by injury to one's body or property.

daybreak   page 90
Daybreak is dawn or when day begins.

dehydrated   page 82
Dehydrated means without enough water.

deltas   page 101
Deltas are large amounts of sand at the mouth of rivers.

desperate   page 18
Desperate means a nearly hopeless situation.

destroyed   page 39
Destroyed means ruined or torn down.

disappearing   page 7
Disappearing is going out of sight.

disturbed   page 32
Disturbed means broke up or upset the order of something.

downstream   page 15
Downstream is the direction in which a body of water, such as a river or a stream, is flowing.

drought   page 47
A drought is a long time without any rain.

earthquake   pages 9, 13
An earthquake is movement or shaking of Earth's crust.

energy   page 93
Energy is power or strength.

erodes   page 101
Erodes is to wear away land. A river erodes land by carrying away rocks and soil.

evaporate   page 85
Evaporate means to remove the wetness from something.

flash flood   page 96
A flash flood is a sudden, dangerous rush of water. It is usually caused by heavy rains.

floodwater   page 49
Floodwater is the water that is in a flood.

flood zone   page 39
A flood zone is an area along a river that can flood when there is a lot of rain.

force   page 64
A force is a strong active power.

fungus   page 82
Fungus is mold or mildew that grows in wet areas.

gale   page 87
A gale is a wind that blows between 32 and 63 miles per hour.

gorge   pages 56, 101
A gorge is a narrow pass that runs between tall, rocky walls.

guides   page 95
Guides are people who lead, teach, or show the way.

gushing   page 79
Gushing means a great amount of water flowing very quickly.

harbor   page 9
A harbor is a place for ships to go where the water is deep and protected from bad weather.

hesitate   page 25
Hesitate means to wait or stop because one is not sure.

horror   page 65
Horror means fear or shock.

huddled   page 73
Huddled means crowded together.

hurricane   page 71
A hurricane is a storm that has very strong winds and usually occurs with rain, thunder, and lightning.

hyenas   page 50
Hyenas are flesh-eating mammals.

hypothermia   page 82
Hypothermia is when a person's body temperature is very low. People in very cold air or water can be in danger of hypothermia.

increase   page 55
Increase means to become greater or more.

infected   page 66
Infected means had a disease that was spread by a germ.

jungle   page 64
A jungle is an area thick with trees and plants.

landslides   page 72
Landslides are large amounts of earth and rock that slide down hills or mountains.

ledge   page 24
A ledge is a rock that sticks out from the side of a hill or mountain and looks like a narrow shelf.

levees   page 77
Levees are the high banks along rivers.

lifeguard   page 25
A lifeguard is a person who works at a beach or a pool to save swimmers from drowning.

life jacket   page 15
A life jacket is a vest or jacket without sleeves that helps a person float on top of the water.

lungs   page 66
Lungs are the organs or parts of the body that breathe air.

map key   page 45
A map key explains what the symbols or colors on a map mean.

mist   page 15
Mist is fine drops of water that float in the air or fall like a very light rain.

moss   page 57
Moss is a soft green plant that grows on rocks, trees, and damp ground.

mouth   page 21
A mouth is the place where a river meets another body of water.

natural disaster   page 42
A natural disaster is a terrible event that is caused by nature, such as a hurricane or a flood.

official   page 95
An official is a person who is in charge.

ordeal   page 82
An ordeal is a painful or terrible experience.

overboard   page 87
Overboard means over the side of a ship into the water.

overflow   page 39
Overflow means to flow over the top, edges, or banks.

oxygen   page 31
Oxygen is a gas that is found in air. Animals and people need to breathe oxygen in order to live.

point of no return   page 57
The point of no return is the place or point beyond which it is not possible to turn back.

poisonous   page 49
Poisonous means causing sickness or death with poison.

polluted   page 42
Polluted means put harmful materials into air, soil, or water.

prowled   page 50
Prowled means quietly wandered around.

rafters   page 55
Rafters are people who float down rivers on rafts.

rainfall   page 47
Rainfall is the amount of rain that falls.

rainstorm   page 71
A rainstorm is a storm with lots of rain.

rapids   pages 16, 21, 61
Rapids are the fast-moving parts of a river.

recovered   page 71
Recovered means regained or returned to normal conditions.

refugee   page 31
A refugee is a person who has had to flee from his or her home to be safe.

regret   page 95
Regret means to be sorry about something.

relax   page 97
Relax means to become less tense or less nervous.

rip current   page 29
A rip current is another name for an undertow. It is water flowing or moving in a particular direction.

riverbank   page 17
A riverbank is the higher ground at the edge of a river.

rogue wave   page 88
A rogue wave is a wave that is much bigger than the waves around it.

ruins   page 50
Ruins are what is left after something has been destroyed.

salt water   page 65
Salt water is water in the ocean.

sandbar   page 29
A sandbar is an area of sand formed by a river or near the shore of an ocean.

scientists   page 10
Scientists are people who are experts in one or more of the sciences.

scrambled   page 48
Scrambled means moved or climbed quickly.

seasick   page 80
Seasick means being or feeling sick from the movement or rolling of waves in the sea.

separated   page 63
To be separated means to be kept apart.

shelter   page 40
A shelter is a place that is covered to keep out such things as rain and snow.

slopes   page 61
Slopes are areas of land that are slanted and not flat.

source   page 21
Source is the place where a river begins.

stalled   page 79
Stalled means stopped moving.

steep   page 88
Steep means slanted in a way that is almost straight up and down.

stilts   page 64
Stilts are long wooden poles.

strait   page 87
A strait is a narrow body of water.

stranded   page 58
A person is stranded if he or she is in a helpless position or is unable to get out of a place.

surf   page 69
Surf is falling waves.

surface   pages 9, 13
A surface is the top layer of something.

surrounding   page 10
Surrounding means circling the area around a place.

survived   page 26
Survived means stayed alive.

survivors   page 34
Survivors are people who stay alive through a disaster, such as a storm or a flood.

swells   page 69
Swells are large waves in the ocean. They do not come to shore.

swirled   page 40
Swirled means moved in circles.

temperature   pages 24, 37
Temperature is how hot or cold something is.

terror   page 89
Terror means great fear.

threatened   page 49
Threatened means gave signs of danger.

thrill   page 16
Thrill means a sudden feeling of excitement.

tidal waves   page 9
Tidal waves are high sea waves along the shore that follow an earthquake.

tides   page 9
Tides are daily movements of the sea toward or away from land.

time bombs   page 34
Time bombs are weapons that can suddenly explode.

torrent   page 47
A torrent is rushing water.

tragedy   page 98
A tragedy is a very unhappy or terrible event.

tropical storm   page 39
A tropical storm is a storm with very high winds and much rain.

tsunami   pages 9, 13
A tsunami is a very large ocean wave that follows an earthquake.

typhoon   page 71
A typhoon is a powerful rainstorm with strong winds.

unconscious   page 26
An unconscious person is one who is not awake.

undertow   pages 24, 29
An undertow is a strong water current that flows away from shore.

upstream   page 96
Upstream is at or toward the beginning of a stream or a river.

vacuum   page 26
A vacuum is a machine that sucks up dirt and dust.

volcanoes   page 31
Volcanoes are holes in Earth's crust that can explode with lava, gases, hot rocks, or ashes.

volume   page 56
Volume means an amount or size.

water cycle   page 53
Water cycle is the movement of water from Earth to the air and then back again.

waterfalls   pages 15, 21, 61, 101
Waterfalls are sudden rushes of rivers over areas that drop.

water vapor   pages 53, 85
Water vapor is water in the form of a gas.

weather map   page 45
A weather map shows the kind of weather to expect in an area.

wet suit   page 95
A wet suit is a rubber suit worn by a swimmer or diver to help keep him or her warm.

white water   page 55
White water is the rough, foamy water found on rivers.

windstorm   page 87
A windstorm is a storm with strong winds and not much rain.

yachts   page 87
Yachts are small ships that are used for racing or pleasure sailing.

zone   page 72
A zone is an area of land.

Did You Know?

◄ Which river floods the most? The Huang He River in China has burst its banks more than 1,500 times over the years. Millions of people have drowned because of the floods, so the river is known as "China's sorrow." In fact, in August 1931, Huang He floods caused the deaths of almost four million people.

Can you believe that the Grand Canyon was once very flat land? It ► took the Colorado River six million years to wash away the land. The running water moved rocks and dirt along until the canyon became very deep and wide. In some places the canyon is more than one mile deep and almost 18 miles wide!

◄ Can you believe that Niagara Falls stopped flowing one time? In March, 1848, an ice jam built up in the Niagara River. This stopped water from flowing over the huge falls. In fact, people could actually walk across the river. After many hours, the river began to flow, and Niagara Falls was a great sight to see again!

What is the world's greatest body of water? The world's largest ocean is the Pacific Ocean. That makes it the greatest body of water on Earth. The Pacific Ocean is bigger than all of Earth's land put together!

◄ Can you believe that some animals can live in rapids? Salmon are very powerful fish that can live in rapids. They leap over the rushing water and travel against the flow of the water. Salmon swim against the river's flow so they can swim to the streams where they were born. There they lay eggs.

Have you ever been inside a cave? Flowing or dripping water makes caves by cutting through rock. Some caves have long, pointed rocks made by dripping water that leaves minerals behind. Rocks that hang from the roofs of caves are called stalactites. Rocks that rise from the floor of a cave are called stalagmites.

CHART YOUR SCORES

Score Your Work

1. Count the number of correct answers you have for each activity.
2. Write these numbers in the boxes in the chart.
3. Give yourself a score (maximum of 5 points) for **Write About It**.
4. Add up the numbers to get a final score for each tale.
5. Write your final score in the score box.
6. Compare your final score with the maximum score given for each story.

Tales	Read and Remember	Think About It	Write About It	Focus on Vocabulary	Science Connection	Score
Big Waves Hit Hawaii						/22
Life and Death at Niagara Falls						/25
Swept Away						/23
The Lake That Kills						/25
Flooding Waters Bury Georgia						/28
Juba River Flood						/23
A Dangerous Sport						/24
Trouble on the Beach						/25
Horror in the Philippines						/23
Survival at Sea						/25
Disaster in Australia						/25
A Dark Wall of Water						/23

ANSWER KEY

Big Waves Hit Hawaii Pages 6–13

Read and Remember — Finish the Sentence:
1. disappear 2. Alaska 3. tower 4. to higher ground 5. lived

Think About It — Find the Main Ideas: 2, 4

Focus on Vocabulary — Match Up: 1. place for ships 2. top layer 3. giant waves 4. shaking of the ground 5. daily movement of sea 6. all around 7. seawater with land partly around it 8. going out of sight 9. people who study science 10. high waves near shore

Science Connection — Giant Waves: 1. Fish flop in the sand. 2. Waves slow down and can become a tsunami when they get near the shore. 3. tsunami 4. up to 165 feet 5. It is highest near shore.

Life and Death at Niagara Falls

Pages 14–21

Read and Remember — Choose the Answer:
1. Jim Honeycutt 2. He couldn't swim. 3. It tipped over. 4. John Hayes's hand 5. He was pulled to safety.

Write About It: Answers will vary.

Focus on Vocabulary — Find the Meaning:
1. jacket that floats 2. fine drops of water 3. into the flowing water 4. places where water drops 5. fast-moving water 6. feeling of excitement 7. moving water 8. box 9. land at a river's edge 10. nearly hopeless

Science Connection — Parts of a River:
1. source 2. bed 3. another body of water 4. its side 5. waterfall

Swept Away Pages 22–29

Read and Remember — Check the Events:
1, 3, 4

Think About It — Cause and Effect: 1. b 2. c 3. d 4. e 5. a

Focus on Vocabulary — Make a Word: 1. cliff 2. ledge 3. lifeguard 4. unconscious 5. crest 6. vacuum 7. temperature 8. undertow 9. survived 10. hesitate. The letters in the circles spell *classmates*.

Science Connection — Ocean Currents:
1. yes 2. rip current or undertow 3. undertow

4. Sandbars are built when a current near the shore moves sand from the beach to the water.
5. A rip current can be dangerous for swimmers because it will pull them into deep water.

The Lake That Kills Pages 30–37

Read and Remember — Finish the Sentence:
1. beautiful 2. soft drinks 3. Lake Nyos 4. exploded 5. cloud of gas

Write About It: Answers will vary.

Focus on Vocabulary — Finish the Paragraphs:
1. volcanoes 2. craters 3. crops 4. disturbed 5. carbon dioxide 6. oxygen 7. creature 8. survivors 9. refugee 10. time bombs

Science Connection — Layers of a Lake:
1. 45–65°F 2. earthworms 3. bottom layer 4. top layer 5. Fish live in the top layer because there is plenty of food.

Flooding Waters Bury Georgia

Pages 38–45

Read and Remember — Choose the Answer:
1. too much rain 2. to his attic 3. food 4. He didn't see them. 5. the 500-year flood

Think About It — Fact or Opinion: 1. F 2. O 3. F 4. O 5. O 6. F 7. O 8. F

Focus on Vocabulary — Finish Up: 1. tropical storm 2. shelter 3. overflow 4. destroyed 5. banks 6. polluted 7. natural disaster 8. swirled 9. barricades 10. flood zone

Science Connection — Weather Map:
1. 🌨 2. rainy 3. Dallas 4. Phoenix 5. Minneapolis

Juba River Flood Pages 46–53

Read and Remember — Check the Events:
2, 3, 6

Write About It: Answers will vary.

Focus on Vocabulary — Crossword Puzzle:
ACROSS — 3. floodwater 6. ruins 7. hyenas 8. torrent 9. scrambled DOWN — 1. prowled 2. drought 4. threatened 5. poisonous 6. rainfall

Science Connection — Water Cycle: 1. the sun's heat 2. clouds 3. wind 4. Water flows into soil, rivers, and oceans. 5. Clouds return water to Earth as rain or snow.

A Dangerous Sport Page 54-61

Read and Remember — Finish the Sentence:
1. helmets 2. rain 3. at the river's edge 4. Green Wall 5. helicopters

Think About It — Drawing Conclusions:
Answers will vary. Here are some possible conclusions. 1. They like the challenge of the rapids. 2. A lot of rain and melting snow flowed into the river. 3. They were in a hurry to get to safety before the river rose more. 4. They wanted to escape the deadly river and were hoping to be rescued.

Focus on Vocabulary — Match Up: 1. people who ride rafts 2. rough, foamy water 3. amount 4. soft green plant 5. units for measuring water 6. stuck 7. make bigger 8. place where one can't turn back 9. place with high walls 10. hard work

Science Connection — The Age of a River:
1. D 2. B 3. B 4. A and D 5. B and C

Trouble on the Beach Pages 62-69

Read and Remember — Choose the Answer:
1. near the ocean 2. a jet engine 3. She got in a canoe. 4. It was washed away. 5. into the mountains

Write About It: Answers will vary.

Focus on Vocabulary — Make a Word:
1. jungle 2. force 3. blur 4. stilts 5. horror 6. infected 7. coastline 8. separated 9. lungs 10. salt water. The letters in the circles spell *north coast.*

Science Connection — Wave Movement:
1. long waves at sea 2. gets higher 3. surf 4. tube 5. back to the ocean

Horror in the Philippines Pages 70-77

Read and Remember — Check the Events:
1, 2, 6

Think About It — Find the Main Ideas: 1, 3

Focus on Vocabulary — Find the Meaning:
1. storm with lots of rain 2. powerful storm with rain 3. level 4. harm 5. strong ocean storm 6. soil sliding down hills 7. crowded together 8. had touched 9. area of land 10. got better

Science Connection — Nature Can Prevent

Floods:
1. A levee is a high bank built of soil left by earlier floods. 2. tree roots 3. A channel is a place where water usually flows. 4. wide channel 5. more likely

Survival at Sea Pages 78-85

Read and Remember — Finish the Sentence:
1. the roof 2. floodwaters 3. salt water 4. duck 5. sunburned

Write About It: Answers will vary.

Focus on Vocabulary — Crossword Puzzle:
ACROSS — 1. seasick 5. fungus 7. dehydrated 8. clung 9. hypothermia DOWN — 2. stalled 3. gushing 4. battered 6. ordeal 8. clump

Science Connection — How Rain Forms:
Sentences should be numbered 2, 3, 1, 5, 4.

Disaster in Australia Pages 86-93

Read and Remember — Choose the Answer:
1. Sydney 2. high waves 3. It sank. 4. a life raft 5. the *Sayonara*

Think About It — Find the Sequence: 4, 1, 5, 2, 3

Focus on Vocabulary — Finish Up:
1. terror 2. yachts 3. steep 4. gale 5. strait 6. abandoned 7. daybreak 8. windstorm 9. overboard 10. rogue wave

Science Connection — Wind and Waves:
1. larger waves 2. crest 3. trough 4. energy 5. in a circle

A Dark Wall of Water Pages 94-101

Read and Remember — Check the Events:
1, 3, 4

Write About It: Answers will vary.

Focus on Vocabulary — Finish the Paragraphs:
1. canyoning 2. wet suit 3. guides 4. canyon 5. official 6. regret 7. upstream 8. flash flood 9. relax 10. tragedy

Science Connection — Water Effects: 1. Fast-moving water wears away a river's bed to form a gorge. 2. where land is steep 3. a wide valley 4. at the mouth of a river 5. Fast-moving water wears away land, riverbeds, and the banks of rivers.